COMPANY MAGAZINE
TOP 100 JOBS

This book is dedicated to each of its readers
with the wish that in your career
you do what you want to do

COMPANY MAGAZINE TOP 100 JOBS

FACTS, CONTACTS AND TACTICS FOR CHOOSING OR CHANGING CAREERS

SUZANNE ASKHAM

VERMILION
LONDON

Published in 1993 by Vermilion
an imprint of Ebury Press
Random House
20 Vauxhall Bridge Road
London SW1V 2SA

Catalogue record for this book is available
from the British Library.

ISBN 0 09 177675 9

Typeset by Hope Services (Abingdon) Ltd.
Printed and bound by
Mackays of Chatham Plc, Kent

CONTENTS

INTRODUCTION TO A BRILLIANT NEW CAREER

Fact: the economy goes up and down but through it all you deserve – and can have – a career to suit you, your personality and your talents. This book will help you to achieve it. You should find its information useful if:

• You are just finishing or have just left school or college and want a first step into an interesting career.

• You have been working for a little while and have a nasty feeling that you're in the wrong career. But you don't know which is the right new job for you. Or how to make the switch.

• Your no-good company has just made you redundant. What can you do next?

• Your current job is OK, but not exactly stimulating. Or perhaps your circumstances are changing – you're having a baby, you're moving town. You want to consider your options, because you know that nowadays people may change careers several times to suit their changing needs. Will something else suit you better?

In the pages that follow you should discover where to find the job to suit you, and how to get it.

Don't be nervous of moving into a new career that looks promising and appealing, but which may turn out not to be right for you. Trust your gut feeling. 'Nowadays, whatever people decide to do is not a decision for life,' points out Derek Kemp, personnel consultant and author of *The Midlife Action Guide*. You'll learn a few skills, and move on. In the end, you have nothing to lose but your overdraft!

'Do what you want to do.' This was the best career advice I was ever given by a school teacher – but in reality, it can be tough to follow your own wishes. There are so many reasons why, in career terms, we find ourselves *not* doing what makes us feel happy and fulfilled. Here are some of them:

• I don't know of any jobs I really want to do.

• I don't have the right qualifications/contacts/luck to get the job of my dreams.

• There are pressures on me – from parents, partners, friends, colleagues, bosses, careers advisers – to follow a particular path.

• I thought I was doing the right thing, but now I realise that I'm not.

All these obstacles are surmountable. With the right information, practical techniques and insider tactics, you *can* get the job you want. You'll find what you need in the 'how to' chapters and – the meat of the book – a directory of the best careers today. The Top 100 Jobs Directory has been compiled by talking to over 500 employers, advisers and, most importantly, happy, successful people who are actually doing the jobs they want to do. They have given inside information on what it's really like to be a professional musician, film editor, venture capitalist, food or fashion buyer . . . and how you can be the same.

Many, like accountants, barristers, nurses, surveyors, vets, are familiar to everyone. Others, like aromatherapists, plant collectors, food stylists, conference organisers, you may not know about at all. These are the ones that careers officers tend not to know much about either, but they happen to be in thriving industries, with wonderful opportunities and rewards.

But even in the most humdrum-sounding career, you can always find exciting, and perhaps unusual options to follow. An accountant, for example, can put millions of pounds to good use in the health service, or balance budgets in a TV station or film studio. Accountancy is a career that allows you to follow your own interests.

TO QUALIFY OR NOT TO QUALIFY?

It's misleading to lay down the law too much where educational qualifications are concerned. Unless you're going for one of the professions – accountancy, architecture, law, medicine etc. – where there's a fixed method of training with set exams at the end, there nearly always is more than one way to get in. People do rise to the tops of their careers without a GCSE or A Level to their name.

Anyone who is short of the odd certificate can progress, if they choose to really go for it. In the Top 100 Jobs Directory, the real need or otherwise for qualifications is made as clear as possible. In something like magazine journalism, for example, though there are training schemes, the fact is that you don't need anything apart from the ability to do the job. In other areas, like engineering, the lack of a degree doesn't stop you from doing the job, but it's a bugbear that you carry through your career, slowing down promotions and new prospects. In one senior engineer's view, the alternative – training on the job – takes longer and may even be more difficult. The same applies to cosmetic science.

Where training is truly optional (as in much of the creative industry) the answer is to take a course if it feels right for you.

Such jobs apart, the consensus among the 500+ people I spoke to was that qualifications are increasingly helpful. 'In a competitive climate, they're a shorthand way of telling employers you've got the brains and general wherewithal to do the job,' says one personnel manager of a large company.

The process of doing a degree or diploma should be enjoyable, useful and is not to be sniffed at. But if you don't want to do one, or feel life's too short, there are alternatives. The new scheme of National Vocational Qualifications means people in all industries will soon be able to acquire skill certificates simply by demonstrating that they can do their jobs.

NVQs are awarded by national examination bodies such as BTEC and City & Guilds. Devised in conjunction with employers in all areas of work, they started up in early 1993. If your current organisation doesn't offer NVQs, get your personnel manager to fix it up – they can start by ringing the NVQ helpline on (0742) 593726. Or ask your local careers office, listed in the phone book under your local authority. In addition, many of the sources listed in the 100 Top Jobs Directory can provide information on on-the-job training.

Note: to get on a degree course you need a minimum of five different subjects in GCSE at grade C or above (including English language and maths), two of which must be at A level – or the equivalent. Mature students – aged twenty-five or over – can get in without the full quota, if they've made achievements in their working lives. It depends on the college, so contact the admissions department of your favoured colleges and ask their advice.

THE RIGHT CLIMATE FOR WORK

In the 1990s it's considered particularly tough to get a job. This is a fact that employers, careers advisers, newspapers, and friends will all be at pains to tell you. Turn their dire warnings into rocket fuel to energise and propel you to the job of your dreams. It is possible. Every day people are walking into exciting, fulfilling careers. You can do the same.

There is a good side to a bad economic climate: because you have to try harder to get the job you want, you quickly develop the mental and physical stamina that will help you, not only to survive, but to thrive in your chosen career. Finding a job can seem about as easy as climbing a rock face . . . but you can do either of those things as long as you learn the appropriate skills, and use the appropriate tools.

The most useful tool of all is a positive attitude. If three rejections fall on to the doormat on the same day, it's natural to take it personally, to think: 'I'm no good/I'll never get a job/the climate's too tough/all employers are vile slugs and I wouldn't want to work for them if they *begged* me.' But the truth is that bitter thoughts will creep like infectious bugs into the next ten applications you write. Employers *hate* coming into contact with a defeatist attitude. They'll reject the sad case and opt instead for someone who sounds able, enthusiastic, motivated, knowledgeable and realistic. To put it another way, Mandi Norwood, who became a magazine editor at twenty-five and is now editor of *Company Magazine*, says, 'Don't ever think the world owes you anything.'

PERSONALITY POWER

Around three-quarters of the people I spoke to while researching this book volunteered the opinion that personality is more important than paper qualifications. When pushed, they defined a good personality as someone who is happy, positive, professional, not scared of hard work, can get on with all sorts of people, has got a sense of humour, and can bring an individual quality to their work.

Because it's so important, the final chapter of this book is devoted to *the psychology of success* and the whole process of presenting your personality to good effect. It's not about changing your character to try and fit in with what's required. As everyone who's tried it has discovered (i.e. most of us), somehow that's never a total success. Our own personalities are powerful beasts, and emerge sooner or later anyway. It's best to take them into account from the start.

HOW TO USE THIS BOOK

The Top 100 Jobs Directory is divided into six sections: Creative and Communications; Great Outdoors and Travel; Influencers; Money, Money, Money; Social Conscience; and Technical Wizardry. By turning to the one-page intro to each section, you'll gain a swift impression of whether that section is for you and you can browse through the individual job descriptions accordingly. And if you want to look up a particular job swiftly, you can turn to the careers index at the back of the book.

But it is also worth skimming through the sections that don't immediately appeal, because there are, for example, travel jobs featuring technical skills, and social conscience jobs that can be downright influential. There may be other careers you have never thought of doing, which turn out to be ideal for you.

Each individual job description will give you condensed facts: you'll get an idea of who you'll be working for; the qualifications and personal qualities required; the salary range; perks and pitfalls; future opportunities; and, most useful, how to get in – the people and organisations to contact.

There's also a thumb-nail sketch of what the career entails, based on interviews with people in each industry to give a sense of what it's like – as well as the low-down on how you can get in, and on, in the same career.

The Top 100 Jobs Directory can be used as a springboard. In the jobs that appeal to you, be really active in following up all the leads outlined. As you go, casually ask family, friends, teachers, colleagues, careers advisers and so on if they know anyone in that industry, for you to talk to. In my research, I was pleased to find that most people like being asked, and they like helping. If someone doesn't want to help, fine, it's up to them; just move on politely and try elsewhere.

And when you get to the applications stage, take a look at the practical chapters at the back of the book, which contain skills and strategies to maximise your chances of getting the job you want.

Everything, including career confidence, comes with practice. To give a simple example, at the start of my writing and editing career, ten years ago, I found the prospect of picking up the phone and talking to total strangers completely intimidating. Practice made it easier, and now, ten years on, I'm a telephone addict.

The same will happen with your *bête noire*, whatever it might be. As Edward de Bono says, 'A difficult task becomes a challenge. A challenge is not a signal for despair but a signal for more information and better thinking.'

So go for it. It's your career, to shape as you choose. It's yours to enjoy. Good luck!

COMPANY MAGAZINE TOP 100 JOBS DIRECTORY

Here it is: your guide to the best careers around today. Browse, skip and dip at will: there's a section for everyone and something in each to suit everyone too!

CREATIVE AND COMMUNICATIONS

Every human being is born creative – we can all feel the satisfaction of using our fertile imaginations to turn an idea into something tangible – a painting, a song, a book, a dress or a dance – and then communicating it to others.

Because we all have the capacity to feel that pleasure, getting a job in the creative sector can be seriously tough. But so what? Competition makes creative people stronger – and more ingenious. Your imaginative brain is your chief asset in dreaming up new ways to break into a creative career. Today: the reception desk at a magazine publishing company . . . tomorrow: the editor's chair?

This is the sector that careers advisers most often misjudge. That's because as a general rule, there are no rules on how to launch yourself into a creative career. Some jobs need training, others don't. Everyone finds the route that works best for them.

For your troubles you'll get long, irregular hours, unglamorous tasks, and if you're one of the many freelance creatives, you'll also get irregular pay. But on the plus side, you'll enjoy a (sometimes) sparkling social life, maybe mixing with the stars, a growing name for yourself . . . and, of course, the satisfaction of seeing that dress collection, that play, that magazine, that chart success, and knowing it was made by . . . you!

ADVERTISING COPYWRITER

Working for: advertising agencies.

Salary range: some start for nothing, otherwise from £9,000 to £60,000 or £80,000; a few have been known to earn £300,000.

Qualifications: not required, though some do degree courses in communications studies, or English. The only thing you need is an ability to produce effective advertising copy, so put together a portfolio of rough ads and ideas. It doesn't matter if you can't draw; the idea's the thing – go for timely campaigns for mainstream products.

Will suit you if you: are creative, communicative, fluent; can work in a team and on your own; are assertive, self-disciplined and keep to the brief.

Perks: doing something creative, imaginative; winning industry awards; larger agencies have spot bonuses, free health club membership; car.

Pitfalls: seriously tough to get in; very stressful once you're in; if you go through a bad run, you're out.

Future opportunities: this industry has been shedding jobs, but there is always room for talented newcomers; later, move on to writing real fiction.

How to get in: • read *Campaign* for industry info • write to companies direct; the aim is to get an appointment with the creative director, and take some ideas you prepared earlier. If you can't get a job, get some work experience of any description • courses info from the industry body, CAM Foundation, Abford House, 15 Wilton Road, London SW1V 1NJ, tel 071–828 7506, 9.30 a.m.–5.30 p.m. If, as an aspiring copywriter, you apply to ad agencies for information on advertising, don't be surprised if they offer you glossy brochures on being one of the money men, *account executives* and media buyers, instead.

The fact is there is no career structure for copywriters. You begin informally, with any work you can get, and you progress informally, being awarded an extremely high salary if the words, slogans and jingles you produce are a success. The only time you ever get formal is when you put on something smart to collect your prize at an industry awards evening.

As a copywriter, you receive a brief from an account executive or manager for each campaign. You'll learn what the product is, who its customers are, whether the client wants the product to appeal more to younger people, go up-market etc. You may do more research yourself, until you get a vivid picture in your mind of the product, and the new image you are going to give it in the public's mind.

You then turn this material into a laser message that will hit the consumers where it matters: their purse. You work closely with the art director, and many ideas will be dreamed up, and thrown out, till you get something that works. After getting an OK from the creative director, you show a rough to the client, and then polish the ad till it's ready for production. You will *dream* slogans.

ARCHITECT/ MODEL-MAKER

Working for: architect practices; developers; local authorities; yourself.

Salary range: £7,000 to £40,000+. Fully-qualified architects, and those in London earn the most.

Qualifications: You do seven years' training, including a degree, a two-year diploma, and two separate years at work. Many practising architects never do the final professional practice exam to become an architect. No qualifications required for model-making, though you need to pick up the skills either at college or on the job; architectural or design training useful.

Will suit you if you: are practical, meticulous, creative; can imagine in 3-D; can sketch; care about the environment; can handle difficult clients.

Perks: get your own fixtures and fittings at trade prices or less.

Pitfalls: recent cutbacks in the building business mean fewer jobs.

Future opportunities: architectural models of every description do have a market. Architects can move into INTERIOR DESIGN or LANDSCAPE GARDENING.

How to get in: • contact the Royal Institute of British Architects, 66 Portland Place, London W1N 4AD, tel 071–580 5533, for free careers booklet including list of schools of architecture • info on model-making and general design courses from The Young Designers Centre, The Design Council, 28 Haymarket, London SW1Y 4SU, tel 071–839 8000, 1.30–5.30 p.m.

Architecture is not a growth area right now, but there are openings for the determined. In a practice, you could be part of a team, working on one major building at a time. You make a survey of the site, and put together a design, making clear how everything will work and how much it will cost. Once the basic design has been agreed you make detailed working drawings. As the building goes up, you may liaise with the builders to iron out any problems. You'll also track down building materials – that could mean anything from selecting a Georgian fireplace from an architectural salvage company to flying out to Italy to choose marble direct from the quarries, as one twenty-nine-year-old architect recently did.

Model-makers produce scale models of anything from a prototype of a medical syringe to the proposed set for a new TV soap. You don't need a designer briefcase full of qualifications – you could be like twenty-four-year-old Bridget Taylor-Sharp who runs her own model-making business, Diminutive Dwellings, together with her husband Lee. 'When I left school I did a six-month secretarial course,' she explains. She did some temping for a design team in an architect's office in Bath, liked it and stayed for eighteen months.

By taking the secretarial route you can pick up knowledge of business practices and model-making techniques, then start up on your own, pitching for commissions from larger companies or private clients. Note: whether you're self-employed or keen to be part of a larger practice, today architects and model-makers alike need to develop good marketing skills.

AUTHOR

Working for: yourself, writing for various publishing houses.

Salary range: peanuts to £100,000+. Most earn £10,000 to £30,000, made up of books income plus other commercial writing (magazine articles, PR material etc.).

Qualifications: none – just evidence you can write in the required style, plus the ability to sell your book or book proposal to an agent or publisher.

Will suit you if you: are self-motivated; have clocked up some unrelated experiences (you need something to write about!); are happy to work on your own; can co-operate with publishers who will want to alter your manuscripts; are full of ideas, a diligent researcher and fluent writer.

Perks: choose your own hours; no boss; get your name on books; library loans bring in extra cash; great opportunities to travel for research.

Pitfalls: you'll work long hours for small advances in the early years.

Future opportunities: the talented, hard-working and lucky can carve out a satisfying career for themselves. Non-fiction is currently much easier to crack than fiction. Profitable area: TV and film script-writing. A low-budget film script can earn you £14,000.

How to get in: • send book proposals direct to suitable publishers – names in the *Writer's Handbook* and the *Writers' and Artists' Yearbook* • read *Writers' Monthly* for tips • get details of Malcolm Bradbury's MA in creative writing from the University of East Anglia, Norwich NR4 7TJ, tel (0603) 56161.

If you want to be a writer, don't be a literary snob, is the message from those who've made it. You could start off as a secretary at a publishers, or survive by contributing articles to business magazines, or work in a bank and write your novel at dawn. Authors come from every imaginable background . . . and all this work experience is data for your writing.

Take Sarah Litvinoff's career. She's done seven books, including relationship guides for Ebury Press. 'At 22 I was a secretary for a book publishing company. Through a colleague I got a job helping the editor for a partwork book (these are generally written by a team of people). I wrote some pieces; she edited them. That's really how I learned my trade.'

You could equally learn it by studying the way other authors write, and by reading up-to-date books on how to write professionally. Basically, you send non-fiction book proposals or complete novels to publishers. If one accepts an idea, they'll give you an advance (anything from £200 to £25,000+). You may earn more later from royalties depending on how many copies are sold.

To supplement your income and hone your skills, you'll take any extra writing jobs you can, sending feature ideas to magazines and following up, if necessary, with an efficient and friendly phone call. And all the time you're collecting snippets and stories from every available source that may trigger a brilliant book idea . . . because dreaming up ideas and turning them into a commercial product is what this business is all about.

BOOK EDITOR

Working for: book publishing companies, in-house or freelance.

Salary range: assistant from £9,000; book editor £12,000 to £30,000+.

Qualifications: many graduates (most do have a degree in this occupation) get in by the secretarial/editorial assistant route so you'll often need appropriate secretarial skills: typing, shorthand. Degrees can be in any subject for non-fiction jobs; English or similar for fiction ones. There are short, optional courses to do before or while in your job – see below.

Will suit you if you: are accurate and check your facts; can spot a potential new Jackie Collins at manuscript stage; are a persuasive talker – you'll deal with designers, accountants, famous and struggling authors.

Perks: free books; launch parties for the famous authors.

Pitfalls: if you make a spelling mistake on the jacket of a book, it'll be read by thousands! Salary is low in the early years.

Future opportunities: jobs have been cut – but the number of books published is still going up, and someone has to edit them. You could become an editorial director, run your own publishing house, become a freelance editor or even, if negotiating contracts is your thing, set up as a literary agent.

How to get in: • career and courses info from Book House Training Centre, 45 East Hill, London SW18 2QZ, tel 081–874 2718, 9 a.m.–5.30 p.m.• see job ads in the *Guardian* on Mondays and Saturdays • one employment agency for secretarial/editorial jobs is Albemarle Appointments, tel 071–499 0092 • write to the personnel departments of publishing houses – the *Writers' and Artists' Yearbook* lists addresses.

A famous thriller writer is on the phone, asking tetchily why his superb 101-word sentence on page 62 has been turned into three shorter chunks. You calm him down, compromise on a couple of minor points. After that call you start to read the typescript of a new novel just handed in by a nervous first-time author. The phone goes: it's the financial director's secretary, asking you for a fast costing of a proposed anthology . . .

Book editing is certainly not all sitting in restaurants, discussing the next great blockbuster – though that happens. As a book editor you will have to negotiate authors' contracts, edit typescripts, send the script for typesetting, read the page proofs for errors. You'll write the blurb to go on the book jacket, discuss the cover with the design department, talk to the publicity manager about how best to promote the book to get as many reviews as possible. And you'll scout, scout, scout for new ideas and new authors.

There are generally more openings on the non-fiction side, but whichever you choose, it's the ability to spot talent that makes an editor's reputation – in this business, you're as good as your authors' sales.

'The best way in is by learning to type,' says one twenty-six-year-old book editor. And from the most humble beginnings you can start making useful contacts.

CATERER

Working for: restaurants, companies and institutions with canteens; hotels; your own catering business.

Salary range: £6,000 to £30,000+.

Qualifications: easiest to get in, and on, with a BTEC, City and Guilds course or degree – the 'classic' training. Good colleges include Oxford, Manchester, and Sheffield polytechnics, and Westminster Catering College.

Will suit you if you: enjoy cooking day after day; don't flap; have drive and energy; are organised; understand business; can charm people.

Perks: free meals; you can work in exotic places; you could serve salmon steaks to royalty, pop stars, actors . . .

Pitfalls: low pay; unsocial hours – you work while others play.

Future opportunities: it's a huge industry and the world is your oyster – especially since they value British finesse abroad. Or set up on your own!

How to get in: • for info/course details contact The Hotel & Catering Training Company, International House, High Street, Ealing, London W5 5DB, tel 081–579 2400 • read *The Caterer and Hotelkeeper* for jobs • Compass employs 20,000 people in everything from directors' lunches to functions attended by royals; you can join them directly from school, then train upwards. Head office is Queen's Wharf, Queen Caroline Street, London W6 9RJ – or phone them on 081–741 1541, 9 a.m.–5 p.m., for regional offices.

There's no shortage of training options in this industry. You can take a hands-on City and Guilds course in cooking; opt for a BTEC diploma and go into management; or do a private course (see the small ads at the back of Harpers & Queen for addresses) and cook for up-market 'do's.

Those in the trade reckon the classic training (C&G, BTEC or degree) will get you into the biggest range of kitchens: college canteens, cheerful wine bars, posh hotels, restaurants and clubs. The salaries offered are low, but tips add up. Sarah, a restaurant manager of twenty-six, is earning £15,000 basic. 'Tips top that to £19,500 a year – if you're pleasant!'

On the business side, you may be in charge of ordering supplies regularly, so your restaurant doesn't run out of vegetables . . . devising a budget for all outgoings, planning promotions like a 'free bottle of wine for romantic couples' evening.

The industrial sector – i.e. directors' dining rooms, institutional canteens, department-store cafés – comes highly recommended by some careers advisers, who say the basic salary is better than in hotels and restaurants. But you might find a restaurant more lively, and your take-home pay ends up around the same. 'Don't be afraid to shop around,' advises catering recruitment consultant Peter Sweeney, 'till you find something that suits you.' See also CRUISE SHIP STAFF.

COSTUME DESIGNER

Working for: BBC, independent TV companies, film and theatre companies – in-house or freelance.

Salary range: £13,000 to £30,000.

Qualifications: people have worked their way up from being a dresser (dressing the actors, mending and ironing their costumes) with no formal qualifications, but employers usually want art/fashion training – Camberwell College of Arts and London College of Fashion are both good, among many others; a degree is the norm at the BBC.

Will suit you if you: are determined, creative, resourceful; are good at tracking down particular items and transporting delicate costumes quickly.

Perks: wonderful travel opportunities; mixing with the stars.

Pitfalls: constantly being on location can ruin your social life.

Future opportunities: openings across the board, but not often advertised, once you're in your first job, you hear about them by word of mouth. The BBC advertises in the national quality papers.

How to get in: • contact BBC Corporate Recruitment, 201 Wood Lane, London W12 7TS, tel 081–752 5252, 9 a.m.–5 p.m. • see job ads in quality papers especially the *Guardian* on Mondays and Saturdays, and in *The Stage* • call wardrobe managers at theatres for wardrobe assistant jobs • ring to make appointments with TV, film and theatre heads of wardrobe to show them your portfolio.

Being a costume designer can take you from the sublime to the ridiculous. You could spend three months on a beach at Cannes, working on a glamorous TV mini-series, or shiver at dawn in a rain-sodden Yorkshire field for a grainy feature film about family tensions. 'This job certainly gives you variety,' says one costume designer in her twenties. 'It's no nine-to-five career.'

It's tough to get in. Tessa Phillips, at thirty-two a freelance designer for the BBC, got her first break in a fairly typical way. After graduating from art school she put together a portfolio – costume drawings she'd done with swatches of fabric attached – knocked on West End stage doors and asked to see the wardrobe manager until she was taken on as a wardrobe assistant. That means ironing, mending clothes, generally looking after them.

To get into TV you might spend two years ringing up heads of costume in BBC and ITV stations, asking if you can show them your portfolio which by now should have a few photos of costumes you helped to design for Jason Donovan, Diane Quick . . . or, more likely, a few extras in a West End play. Sometimes the heads don't even open your portfolio. Don't give up though.

Once you've got your first TV or film job, your energy is devoted to producing perhaps 200 costumes for a particular series. Every detail must be correct, which means checking facts in museums such as the V&A. You design, get the garments made, hire or buy others. You might even go shopping with your stars. On location, you're responsible for ensuring that every item is there when it's needed. 'To get on as a costume designer it's no good waiting to be told what to do if things go wrong – it's up to you to do it,' says Tessa. And that starts with your first job hunt.

DANCER

Working for: dance companies; dance schools; your own company or school.

Salary range: £6,000 (or less) to £12,000+. Stars earn much, much more. Dancers get living allowances on tour.

Qualifications: Depending on the dance course you do, you may need no previous qualifications, or you may need to hold amateur dance certificates. You may also need anything up to two A Levels. Ballet dancers invariably have started training from early teens.

Will suit you if you: have natural grace, a sense of rhythm, a flexible and fit body, and stamina; are imaginative, self-disciplined and can take hard work.

Perks: you'll develop a graceful dancer's physique; the chance to travel.

Pitfalls: you're unlikely to become wealthy; your active dancing career will be finished by your mid- to late thirties, earlier in ballet.

Future opportunities: qualified, experienced dancers can become dance teachers, dance therapists, theatre administrators . . .

How to get in: send a large SAE for accredited courses and funding info to The Council for Dance Education and Training, 5 Tavistock Place, London WC1H 9SS • send for prospectus for ballet courses from The Royal Academy of Dancing, 36 Battersea Square, London SW11 3RA • prospectus for contemporary dance courses from The Contemporary Dance Trust, 17 Dukes Road, London WC1H 9AB, tel 071–387 0152 • read *The Dancing Times* for jobs and industry info.

The good news for would-be contemporary dancers is that you don't need to have been practising pirouettes from the age of twelve as ballet dancers invariably do. Contemporary dancers can start training without a single amateur dance certificate as late as eighteen, but sixteen or seventeen is the norm. One of the best places to go is The London Contemporary Dance School. 'No dance qualifications are needed to apply,' confirms a spokesman (though a mix of GCSEs and A Levels is generally required, depending on the course). Everyone who applies gets an audition. He adds that it's vital you know what you're letting yourself in for: this is a tough, low-paying career. Along with the classes you'd expect – ballet, body conditioning, choreography, history of dance, and music – you'll also be entering competitions in the hope of winning a prize that will help you gain a good dance company place.

Isabel Tamen, twenty-nine, trained at the above school and has danced her way across Britain and in Paris in a small company. Today she's at the Contemporary Dance Theatre. In a big company like that, you'll earn about £290 a week, doing a range of dances, with extra living allowances when you go on tour. 'You have to be totally committed because it tends to dominate your life,' says Isabel. The contacts you develop through your dance school, plus regular reading of the trade press, should keep you up to date with jobs. For well-paid work such as TV shows, it's unusual to get in without some stage experience. Contact the shows and TV stations direct – addresses in *The Official ITV Careers Handbook*. See also CRUISE SHIP STAFF.

FASHION/TEXTILE/ KNITWEAR DESIGNER

Working for: clothing and fabric manufacturers; yourself.

Salary range: £7,000 to £35,000+; for those who own their own big businesses, the sky's the limit.

Qualifications: take your pick according to what feels right for you: it's common to do a three-to-four-year degree course, with time out in industry, or a BTEC diploma. Range of subjects available includes fashion/ textiles; design (fashion); knitwear design. You can also do a Masters degree. A small number of companies such as Joe Bloggs take school-leavers with no fashion experience, simply a knowledge of club styles; and a number of successful designers have no formal training at all.

Will suit you if you: are creative, original, commercial, and practical; are interested in all aspects of fashion; have business skills.

Perks: work your own hours, work where you choose; see your designs on the cover of a magazine or on people in the street.

Pitfalls: the fashion industry hasn't been too profitable in recent years; if you contract out some of the work, such as dying, manufacturing, keep an eye on the quality control – one big reason why some new companies go bust.

Future opportunities: what you make of them. With good products, and the marketing skills to get them to the buyer, you can flourish within a few years.

How to get in: contact The Design Council, 28 Haymarket, London SW1Y 4SU, tel 071–839 8000 • Careers Information Service, CAPITB, 80 Richardshaw Lane, Pudsey, Leeds LS28 6BN, tel (0532) 393355 • shop carefully for the right course: there's a range of names which cover a multitude of things • for industry info, read *Drapers Record*.

'You have to be fairly commercial, but I think it's important to do your own thing, not be too much part of a fashion crowd,' says Frances Slater, who owns her own business with a partner in the Scottish Highlands. Their silk and linen clothing with chameleon panels are sold in shops like London's Hyper Hyper, and will shortly be sold in Japan.

And that's probably the crux of it. You can take the more secure and less exciting route, by applying for a job in a big business, such as one of the many suppliers who create classics for Marks and Spencer . . . or you can be bold and go it alone.

If you do the latter, you need a USP, a unique selling point, to distinguish yourself from the thousands of other hopefuls who emerge from college each year. That means being absolutely aware of what is going on in fashion all around you, but not being unduly influenced by it; instead, developing your own trademark style, and once you've done that; making sure you get publicity by sending photos and information to magazines, and samples of your clothing to retailers. In the early years, good accountancy advice and going for business grants can be crucial.

FEATURES EDITOR ON A MAGAZINE

Working for: magazine publishing companies.

Salary range: £12,000 to £30,000

Qualifications: formal ones generally not important: about half of all journalists have a degree (in any subject). There are magazine journalism courses – two good places are City University, London, and the London College of Printing. Train if it feels right for you. But these informal skills are vital: being tenacious, a fluent communicator, able to turn complicated jargon into understandable, concise, contemporary English.

Will suit you if you: enjoy the whole process of turning the raw material of everyday living into readable stories; can empathise with all types of different people; can work quickly and for long periods; are a teamworker, sociable, curious, analytical, creative, accurate, and don't give up.

Perks: free trips to exotic places; other freebies like film premières, review copies of books, foods, make-up etc. (depending on your magazine).

Pitfalls: hard to get in; if your magazine is sold to another house, or folds (closes), your job could go too; long hours with no overtime pay.

Future opportunities: once you've learned your trade, you have a marketable skill you'll never lose: you can be an editor, then possibly publisher, move across to newspapers, launch your own magazine, become a freelance writer or editor.

How to get in: • read magazines constantly, and familiarise yourself with how they're put together – how could they be improved? • read all newspapers, not just your favourites, to develop your news sense • apply direct to the editor/features editor of magazines you like for a junior job, work experience, anything • two useful directories for employers' names and addresses are: the *Writers' and Artists' Yearbook* and *The Media Guide* • job ads in the *Guardian* on Mondays • read *UK Press Gazette* and *Private Eye* for some inside info • shop around for courses, if you want.

'If you're a features editor, or an assistant in that department, you have to produce the goods every time,' says Tara Barker, deputy editor/features on *Company Magazine*. This means producing an article to the right brief, the right length, with the right style . . . and then doing it again tomorrow, and the next week. Some articles can be difficult to research: if you're investigating say, a scandal in the construction industry, people may tell you they don't know anything about it. Don't give up. Keep ringing, asking people in a friendly, knowledgeable fashion, and someone will eventually give you your scoop.

Features editors are in charge, under the editor and with the help of the features team, of dreaming up feature ideas, then either commissioning freelance journalists, or doing the articles in-house. You will develop a good, wide-ranging list of contacts. You have to locate facts fast, report them accurately, and in an appropriate tone for the readers and the subject. And the initiative you need for that is precisely the same initiative you need to get a job in the first place.

FILM EDITOR

Working for: film, video and TV production companies, increasingly as a freelance.

Salary range: from £20,000 to £30,000+; minimum union rate, £460.50 per week.

Qualifications: none is usually required except good colour vision, manual dexterity, ability to do the job or to learn it (TV companies have some trainee editing schemes). You can do a film course (see below) and/or join a production company as a 'runner' – literally, fetching and carrying everything from tea to film reels, learning as you go.

Will suit you if you: have a real interest in photography and film-making; pay attention to details; are creative, organised, and can work under pressure.

Perks: you're the one who shapes the final film.

Pitfalls: long, irregular hours and irregular income.

Future opportunities: the hot competition for jobs means a pruning process takes place. If you stick at it and acquire the necessary skills, there's regular work. You need to adapt to changing technology and opportunities such as the growth of satellite and cable TV. Or you can move into directing, writing etc.

How to get in: • The British Film Institute, 21 Stephen Street, London W1P 1PL have useful books e.g. *Film & Television Training* (£4.24 inc. p&p) • The National Film and Television School, Beaconsfield Studios, Station Road, Beaconsfield, Bucks HP9 1LG runs courses for people with some film experience • courses list from British Kinematograph Sound & Television Society, M6–14 Victoria House, Vernon Place, London WC1B 4DF • contact film companies direct • see also TV RESEARCHER • read *Screen International* • network!

Editing is the most invisible part of film-making, the part that turns a collection of jumbled-up and over-long film sequences into an interesting, logical and seamless story.

It's a real behind-the-scenes job that takes place in the cutting room. After the film has been shot, you view the whole disorganised film with the director, and decide which bits should be cut, which need putting into order. Some directors then leave you to get on with it – which gives you the most responsibility and creativity. Others don't.

Film, as opposed to video, is used for feature films, and good-quality TV dramas and documentaries; all the rest is done on video. When you're editing film, you physically cut it, while you edit video tape by recording the good bits in sequence on to another tape.

Film editing involves much more simple equipment, and more skill from you: you run long ribbons of film through a small viewing machine, and cut out individual frames or long sequences. You stick separate strips of film together with tape or special adhesive. Your assistant takes each strip of film and makes a record of what's on it, so you can find it again when you want to attach that moving reunion between two lovers to the end of the car-chase scene . . . or whatever else the storyline, and you, as editor, decide.

FLORIST

Working for: someone else's florist shop, or, later on, your own.

Salary range: YTS trainees £35 per week; then £6,500 to £13,000.

Qualifications: none required. Commonest route in is as an apprentice, often on a Youth Training Scheme: apply to florists whose work you admire. Alternatively you can do a college diploma – City and Guilds either full-time or on block-release from a florist's shop. The Welsh College of Horticulture is good.

Will suit you if you: are creative; can add up swiftly in your head; are good at listening and communicating with clients; are unflappable under pressure.

Perks: spending your days surrounded by flowers is pleasurable; some free flowers and plants.

Pitfalls: you are most unlikely to get rich.

Future opportunities: the motivated and ambitious can progress: you could set up on your own, perhaps specialising in photo shoots or society events where famous brides clutch your bouquets!

How to get in: • send A5 SAE to British Retail and Professional Florists' Association, Roebuck House, Newbury Road, Hermitage, Newbury, Berks RG16 9RZ • send large SAE to Lynda Trompetto ICSF, Society of Floristry, 70a Reigate Road, Epsom, Surrey KT17 3DT • prospectus from Welsh College of Horticulture, Northop, Mold, Clwyd CH7 6AA, tel (0352) 86861.

'I want an arrangement one metre high by nearly two metres across to go on a sideboard for a formal business function,' says a lady on the other end of the phone. As the florist, you have to make some instant, informed calculations in your head, and come up with an estimate of how much it will cost – customers are inclined to go elsewhere if you dither.

This career is not just about arranging roses and Gypsophila prettily in wicker baskets – though that is a pleasurable part of it. You need to pick up, on the job, a string of business skills such as keeping accounts, and calculating the correct profit margins on stock. You'll also need to be good at dealing with vague customers, building up a workable idea in the space of a brief conversation.

Florists often start work early, at 8 a.m. or so. You'll be sourcing the flowers and plants that you need to fill orders: some suppliers come to you, other flowers you order by rail from Covent Garden. 'It's important to build up a number of reliable suppliers,' says one florist aged twenty-seven. 'You're looking for the best and the cheapest. The nightmare is when you've got a major order for a wedding and a supplier hasn't produced the goods – you must speedily locate something suitable from another supplier.'

Florists agree that it's beneficial to train all the way through your career. The ultimate accolade is the Society of Floristry diploma: you study while working, taking about five years to get the grade.

FOOD STYLIST/ ECONOMIST

Working for: mainly book publishers, magazines, food producers, ad agencies, in a freelance capacity.

Salary range: assistants £40 per day; stylists £160 to £300+ per day, up to £50,000+ per year (editorial pays less than advertising, but has most kudos).

Qualifications: a home economics or catering course (see address below for details); entry requirements depend on the actual course.

Will suit you if you: love food, are imaginative, have a good eye, can work under pressure.

Perks: a creative job in a sociable industry; no boss.

Pitfalls: long, irregular hours; dealing with often indecisive clients.

Future opportunities: once you're in, there is plenty of work – especially doing photos for supermarket food packaging.

How to get in: • careers and courses info from Institute of Home Economics, Aldwych House, 71–91 Aldwych, London WC2B 4HN, tel 071–404 5532 • study food pics in magazines and books and check the credits by the photos to see who did the food styling. Contact food stylists whose work you admire (ask the magazine and book art departments, try the Institute of Home Economics, or look them up in a London residential directory), then ring them and ask if you can do some work experience with them.

'I'm a home economics graduate who wants to go into photographic styling; I've seen your work in X Magazine; can I come in and help you,' is a request that should get some results if put to an established food economist/food stylist.

Food styling and home economics in this field are the same job – food stylist is simply the trendier name, but whether you call yourself one or the other, you'll have a home economics training. A general stylist, on the other hand, is no foodie, but tracks down the props – crockery, candlesticks and other non-food items – required to give the shot a suitable ambience. (But these general stylists are sometime called food stylists!)

This is the way the industry works: an art director/art editor commissions a photographer to produce some pictures for a magazine article, a book, or, very commonly, the latest new frozen food from a supermarket. The photographer decides on which food stylist he wants to use (the art editor may also have an opinion), so, it makes sense to get to know the photographers. You may have found a staff job in a food company, and gained in-house experience of helping to produce photos. Or you could apprentice yourself to established food stylists. Whichever, in this sociable industry, talk to the photographer, and the assistant – the assistant will eventually become a photographer; you could make a good team.

You'll cook up the food in the studio and get it ready at exactly the right moment, so that omelettes are still bubbling and roasts glisten. The studio is sometimes invaded by clients who turn up and change their mind half-way through. You'll develop calm nerves, tact and a certain presence.

HAIR STYLIST: CUTTER/TECHNICIAN

Working for: hair salons throughout UK.

Salary range: juniors on £50 to £70 per week, YTS trainees on £35. When qualified: £150 to £200 per week. Top stylists get around 30 per cent of the fee for each haircut or treatment they do.

Qualifications: you go in to a salon as a junior and do a three-year training scheme on the job. No qualifications required at the start, but you should have a sense of style that fits in with the salon's. And do apply to the top salons: they try to look at everything that comes in, and there is a high turnover of juniors, so you always stand a chance. Or do a course, at a local college or a private school – e.g. Vidal Sassoon in London or Manchester.

Will suit you if you: really care about the subject and see it as a career, not just a job; are in tune with fashion; are willing to work hard; have a good visual eye and colour sense; have a pleasant manner.

Perks: in top salons, the chance to get your work in the glossies; cut the hair of the rich and famous; tips.

Pitfalls: standing up all day long; handling noxious hair treatment chemicals such as peroxides.

Future opportunities: hair-cutting is a skill you'll always be able to use; set up as a freelance stylist, travelling to people's homes; or hit the CRUISE SHIPS and travel the world.

How to get in: • careers and courses info from The Hairdresser Training Board, 3 Chequer Road, Doncaster DN1 2AA, tel (0302) 342837 • prospectus from Vidal Sassoon Schools Administration, 15 Davies Mews, London W1Y 1AS, tel 071–629 5686 • contact direct the hair salons that appeal to you • see job ads in *Hairdressers Journal International*. • learn all you can about hair and fashion – develop a feel for emerging trends.

'I'd rather someone came to us with no hair-cutting experience at all,' says one top London salon manager. 'That way we know they won't have any bad habits; we'd rather train them ourselves.'

So it's worth contacting the salons before you do anything else. In a salon that cares about training, and structures it properly (make sure yours does before you start), it's the best option since the training is free and you have a job at the end of your three years.

The first weeks are spent doing lowest-of-the-low tasks: sweeping the floor, making tea, watching your older colleagues at work. Gradually, the work becomes more advanced. You have evening training sessions during which you cut volunteers' hair under supervision, and learn the principles of colouring and bleaching.

When you're qualified you may specialise as a cutter, or as a technician – doing perms, colouring, wacky designs for fashion shows and the odd magazine shoot. But everyone in the trade agrees that a hairstyle works better if the technician and the stylist are both all-rounders: you each specialise in one, but understand the other.

INTERIOR DESIGNER

Working for: a design consultancy; yourself.

Salary range: £7,000 to £60,000+

Qualifications: you can get into this industry by doing up someone's house, and then another, or by learning the trade with an established designer – but nowadays the majority of people starting out have a qualification, preferably a degree (Kingston University, Chelsea College of Art and Design are both good). A BTEC diploma is also fine.

Will suit you if you: have an eye for design and colour; are adept at making contacts (much business comes through word of mouth); have an understanding of architecture; can track down required items.

Perks: meet a few rich and famous; furniture and fitting at trade prices.

Pitfalls: hard, physical work; tight schedules; clashes between the clients' taste and your own.

Future opportunities: you'll have to be very determined – there are currently few jobs. Once in, your future is as good as your last design.

How to get in: • send an A4 SAE to The Interior Decorators and Designers Association, Crest House, 102–104 Church Road, Teddington, Middx TW11 8PY for further info • contact notable interior designers for jobs – this is a field where the secretary can become an assistant designer . . .

'The best things about this job are being able to do something creative, and getting out and about,' reckons Gilly Chance, who runs her own design consultancy and employs two assistants.

She and other designers say the worst aspect is the sheer amount of hard work, and it's a myth that interior designers always 'know' exactly the look to go for. 'You can agonise for hours.'

Shop around for a course to suit you, but make sure it teaches computer-aided design: paint your colour schemes on the computer screen. CAD skills are much sought after by employers – the computer avoids expensive mistakes like decking a room out in blue only to realise it looks terrible.

As a designer, you need to decide on lighting, heating, paint finishes, windows, tiles, kitchens, bathrooms, everything – carpets and curtains are only the garnish to your creation – then track down and get installed the items you have chosen. You'll be dealing with fixtures and fittings wholesalers, builders, architects, and the client, all with strong and different views. So the ability to talk persuasively is vital.

Today, you'll almost certainly work for a design consultancy, someone else's or, after a few years, your own. To see how employment patterns have changed, look at the fun area of show houses on new estates, where the designer does them up to tempt the buyer. In the property boom, building developers had whole design teams on their staff. Today, many have been laid off, and freelance design consultants are hired as required. Enter Gilly Chance and her team. And enter, possibly, you.

JEWELLERY DESIGNER

Working for: yourself; a large jewellery manufacturer.

Salary range: £5,000 to £20,000+ depending on your sales. Low income in the early years.

Qualifications: none strictly required if self-employed; those going into jewellery manufacturing (broadly, less creative but steadier income) should contact firms direct for information – many train while employed. But best way for self-employed designers to learn is through a two- to four-year course, a degree or BTEC HND in 3-D design with jewellery options: check that the college you choose is in touch with the commercial world, and covers your interests.

Will suit you if you: love making things; are an original thinker, ingenious, practical, manually dextrous, patient; have good business sense.

Perks: seeing your latest design being worn by someone in the street; being your own boss.

Pitfalls: unsteady income, could feel isolated.

Future opportunities: jewellery-wearing is never out of fashion, so with the right attitude and aptitude, a satisfying long-term career; teach it too.

How to get in: • send an SAE for good careers, courses, grants info to The Crafts Council, 44a Pentonville Road, London N1 9BY, tel 071–278 7700, 10 a.m.–6 p.m. • courses info from The Design Council, 28 Haymarket, London SW1Y 4SU, tel 071–839 8000 • immerse yourself in the subject to gain a sense of your market place: study fashion magazines, *Crafts* magazine, books, exhibitions.

Imagine yourself in your own studio in an old converted school or warehouse. Along the corridor are other designers and makers, of pottery, jewellery, architectural models, commercial illustration, so you don't feel isolated, and you can pool some useful resources, such as a fax machine and photocopier.

You may specialise in silver, gold, acrylic, paper, base metals. You develop new jewellery designs, first in your head, then on paper, and ultimately using your small range of valuable equipment: a work bench, rolling mills (a mangle for rolling out sheets of metal), metal cutters, machines to polish metal or stones.

If you're motivated you can establish a fulfilling career for yourself designing and making jewellery to commission and for sale in shops. It's expensive to begin with, but there are grants available from the Crafts Council which awards up to £7,500 to new businesses, the Enterprise Allowance Scheme, and the Princes Youth Trust if you're under twenty-six.

'It's vital to publicise your work,' advises Alison Evans who creates stunning silver jewellery in her Brighton workshop. 'Take colour slides of your work, and send them to magazines. The more you appear in magazines, the more your work sells.' Taking a small stand at suitable trade fairs is an effective way of reaching the maximum number of retailers, and journalists.

MAKE-UP ARTIST

Working for: yourself, doing work for magazines, newspapers, books, advertising and fashion shows, film, TV, stage.

Salary range: magazines: £50 to £150 per day; ads, PR, catalogue work: £300 to £400 per day. At the start you'll work around three days a week, but once established, every day. On longer contracts for TV etc.

Qualifications: none required; many private courses expensive and bad. London College of Fashion has some good courses. TV or stage artists more likely to need BTEC diploma or similar. Most magazine/advertising make-up artists train on the job.

Will suit you if you: have a strong sense of style, fashion, colour, light; understand the photographic process; are out-going, friendly, reliable and fast.

Perks: get close to famous faces; some free make-up.

Pitfalls: hard to get established; long hours; late payments.

Future opportunities: a very profitable area if you make it.

How to get in: • courses info from London College of Fashion, School of Fashion Promotion, 20 John Prince's Street, London W1M 0BJ, tel 071–629 9401; or shop around for BTEC courses local to you • study magazines etc. and contact the make-up artists whose work you admire (through their beauty editor/agent/London residential phone directory/*The Knowledge*, available in libraries); ask if you can help them and learn • read *Allure*, an American magazine which shows current make-up methods in detail.

'You do get people turning up who aren't with an agency, but they're not as together. Agencies make sure they're doing it all properly, right down to the portfolio,' explains one magazine health and beauty editor.

So, to get work you need an agent, but to get an agent you need work, because agents are too busy to train artists from scratch. Kirsta Madden, co-owner of make-up artists' agency Time Management, recommends the following: go and get training if you want to, but realise that this is a very fast-moving area and tutors can slip out of touch unless they're still working as make-up artists.

The most important thing is to get a job as an assistant in any capacity to an established make-up artist who will take you along on jobs. In between making tea and fetching sandwiches, you'll learn invaluable inside knowledge on how to make models look flawless on film.

Then, get together with a photographer's assistant and a fashion assistant (you'll meet these on shoots). The latter will get the clothes, the former will take the pics, you'll do the make-up . . . and you'll have some decent images for your portfolio. Agents do take people on at that stage. Another idea is to ring up beauty editors on the weeklies and ask if you can do the make-up for those articles in which readers are given a brand new image with the help of expert make-up and fashion advice. You won't get paid much, but it's good for your portfolio. This field is seriously competitive but as long as you don't give up, you could be established within two or three years.

MODEL

Working for: yourself, through an agent, doing a mix of magazine and advertising work and – the staple of many models' work – fashion catalogues. Also some work in fashion houses.

Salary range: variable, from peanuts to a hell of a lot. Day rate for photographic work: £250 to £400+ per day. Most models on £15,000 to £20,000.

Qualifications: no formal ones required. You can do a reputable course, e.g. the one-year certificate course at the London College of Fashion – but courses do not lead to a job.

Will suit you if you: have good, regular, photogenic features; are at least 5' 8" tall, are more or less 34–24–34; fit in with current or developing tastes (at present slim but curvy, black or mixed blood, or pale waifs); are persistent and well-disciplined; have stamina; can hold your own in a tough environment; aren't self-conscious about your body.

Perks: some discounts on clothes; travel to exotic places.

Pitfalls: you'll face the bimbo factor – people assuming you're dumb; having to spend a lot on clothes to look the part; variable income.

Future opportunities: you could run your own model agency afterwards, or teach, or become a fashion journalist if you can prove your writing skills.

How to get in: • contact The London College of Fashion, 20 John Prince's Street, London W1M 0BJ, tel 071–629 9401 • approach reputable model agents direct, bearing in mind you'll probably get lots of rejections before one accepts you.

Hours of waiting in a dingy studio, make-up and hair done . . . then a sudden need for speed. Shrugging into outfits, one after another after another, having hair and make-up adjusted and then switching on the glamour in front of the camera, acting whatever part is required. 'Even if you don't like the clothes you have to pretend they're stunning, and you're glamorous,' says one model. Your mood projects on to the resulting pictures. Models who can do this are the ones who make it – as long as you have the right physical shape.

Somewhere along the line you will have learned how to move gracefully (or maybe you're a natural). What you won't have done is gone on an expensive private course. Here is the advice of the Association of Model Agents in London, whose members include the best model agencies like Elite Premier, Models One, and Storm:

First, contact reputable agencies with one or two photos of yourself: one of your face, another showing your shape. The agencies can tell you on the spot whether, in their view, you will make it. Never answer an ad for would-be models. Don't put your own portfolio together, because until you're actually in the business, you can never know the best way to do it. An unprofessional portfolio is screamingly obvious to the art directors who hire models. Once you're accepted by an agency, they will help you provide a really strong, effective portfolio. 'There are only about 200 girls making a living as models in London,' says one member of the Association. If you don't have the physical shape, you can't change it, but you can move into a related field that appeals.

MUSICIAN/SINGER

Working for: yourself, on contract to record companies when you make it.

Salary range: from less than nothing (you pay to play) to . . . the sky's the limit. The Musicians' Union tries to establish fair rates for gigs: e.g. London minimum £31.50 to £58 per night depending on the size of the venue.

Qualifications: just the ability to play an instrument/sing well and a total determination to succeed. Many musicians train on one or two instruments, then do their own thing. People train as much or as little as feels right for them.

Will suit you if you: are obsessed with succeeding, love your music and practise every day; have a stubborn belief in yourself; have a commercial sense; are open to new styles and trends; are sociable (know those talent scouts).

Perks: you could be a star!

Pitfalls: irregular pay in the early years; smoky, airless working conditions; on tour – exhausting and expensive – relationships may suffer.

Future opportunities: non-stars or ex-stars go into assorted jobs in the music industry. These include working as an A&R manager or band manager, into music admin., session music/singing, music therapy or teaching music.

How to get in: • info from The Musicians' Union, 60/62 Clapham Road, London SW9 0JJ, tel 071–582 5566, 9.30 a.m.–4.45 p.m. • read *Melody Maker* for info/session jobs etc. • if you need a band, put ads up in good local music shops • don't stay at home! Play or watch others play every night.

What every musician really wants to know is: what is it about the people who make it . . . what is so special about *them*?

'Be different, be organised and keep at it,' is Tim Rice's advice. Singer and keyboards player Lucia Holm puts it another way: her band Sunscreem first reached the charts in '92 and they released their first album at the start of '93 under the Sony Soho Square label. 'We've got an awful lot of songs, and we're not trying to be anyone else – we're being ourselves. The band has a lot of strong personalities in it.'

They also worked their butts off. Lucia is not alone in having done undemanding day jobs – gardening, house-cleaning – in order to play: there are so many musicians trying to scramble from amateur to professional status that pubs and clubs often charge bands for the privilege of playing.

On the positive side musicians say the music industry is quite small if you immerse yourself in it at this level; you do get to know the talent scouts, you do meet someone who wants to be your manager . . . and who sort of knows someone at a record company. . . . The steps forward are imperceptible, but if you stick at it you do progress. Lucia's band caught the attention of EMI, who couldn't quite decide. But that alerted other companies, and the band was signed up. Why shouldn't the next one be you?

PAINTER/ILLUSTRATOR

Working for: yourself, usually, to commissions from private individuals and businesses: e.g. magazines, book publishers, greeting card companies, or selling through art galleries.

Salary range: what you make it, from £4,000 to the sky's the limit. A single book cover illustration would earn you from £250 to £650.

Qualifications: none required but many artists first do degree courses in fine art, or illustration. Entry conditions to these vary. Or you can do a BTEC diploma course which has a greater commercial emphasis (the degree courses focus more on creativity and developing an individual style). No two courses are the same, and not everyone feels the need for formal training; some train on the job in design studios or advertising agencies alongside the advertising copywriter. It's useful today for illustrators to know a bit abut typography and desk top publishing (DTP).

Will suit you if you: are strongly motivated; are creative, original, imaginative with a good visual eye; are practical, can work on your own but have a social network to stop you getting isolated; have a positive attitude dealing with clients; have good business and marketing sense.

Perks: opportunities to travel where your art takes you; painting some famous faces; being your own boss; becoming famous.

Pitfalls: sometimes working very long hours; irregular and late payments.

Future opportunities: what you make of them: attitude and ability are all-important; you can teach, do art therapy, be an AGENT/gallery owner.

How to get in: • careers and courses info from The Association of Illustrators, 29 Bedford Square, London WC1B 3EG, tel 071–636 4100 • shop around for the best courses to suit you – ask for prospectuses, visit colleges and talk to artists whose work you admire • read the *Writers' and Artists' Yearbook* for market info on selling your work • read *The Artist's and Illustrator's Magazine* for exhibitions and industry info.

To get work you need to show the work you've already done – even if you haven't yet had a single commission. Enter the portfolio: that glossy, well-presented advertisement of what you can do.

Shops that sell artists' and designers' equipment have a good range of big plastic folders with sleeves: you put in examples of your work – book cover and greeting cards illustrations, advertising ideas, photos of paintings – whatever your interests are, mounted on black or coloured paper. You make them look mainstream and commercially viable, and as you get real commissions you put published cuttings of those works prominently at the front.

Art directors and the others who commission illustrators are always interested in seeing new work. So ring, or write to them – on paper with a distinctive letterheading designed by you (see LETTERS THAT WORK FOR YOU) – and fix up appointments. Some work experience in an illustrators'/design studio is useful for honing commercial skills and getting some work published, which will help you to attract your first paid-for commissions.

PHOTOGRAPHER

Working for: yourself, to commissions from books, magazines, newspapers, ad agencies, or your own high street business; large organisations.

Salary range: £8,000 to £100,000+; ed/ad day rates, approx £250 to £400. High street business: £20,000 to £30,000.

Qualifications: you need to learn your trade; whether you do this at college or working as a junior/assistant with a photographer is up to you.

Will suit you if you: have a good eye, a sense of composition, technical understanding; are imaginative, resourceful, flexible; make others feel at ease.

Perks: being your own boss.

Pitfalls: income is very erratic; late payments.

Future opportunities: what you make of them; if you have the right temperament and expertise, you can specialise in portraits, sport etc.

How to get in: • approved college courses info from British Institute of Professional Photography, Fox Talbot House, Amwell End, Ware, Herts SG12 9HN, tel (0920) 464011 9 a.m.–5 p.m. (A5 SAE preferred) • The Association of Fashion Advertising & Editorial Photographers gives careers talks once a month: 9–10 Domingo Street, London EC1Y 0TA, tel 071–608 1441 • study photos in mags, books, exhibitions etc.; contact photographers whose work you admire and ask for an assistant's job, work experience • take your portfolio to the art directors of publications (addresses in the *Writers' and Artists' Yearbook*).

'You make the most of any openings you get,' says one photographer, explaining the haphazard way a freelance photographer becomes established. 'One of the many, many art directors I showed my work to asked me to do a book cover of a celebrity. A magazine then wanted to use the picture, so instead of just sending them a copy, I went in, said hello to them and showed them my portfolio. They liked the work, and commissioned me to do other things for them.'

And so it goes. In the early years of being a freelance photographer you will tout your portfolio – of published and unpublished pictures – to hundreds of art directors. Ideally, with or without college experience, you will have first found a position as assistant to a successful pro. This lowly job entailing equipment carrying, light metering, and making endless cups of coffee is a brilliant way to pick up tricks of the trade. You find out how to get work, how to bill for it, how to make subjects natural. You could also, however, start off on your own from day one.

Editorial and advertising are not the only openings for photography, of course, though they can be the most profitable. You could join the colour laboratory of a large manufacturing company, the health service, the Armed Forces, the police (recording the scene of a crime). Or you could take commissions for portraits of private individuals: the high street business. If you have the right friendly, go-getting manner, you could make a name for yourself locally as the person for baby pictures or weddings.

PICTURE RESEARCHER

Working for: magazines, newspapers, book publishers, photo agencies.

Salary range: £9,000 to £20,000 on magazines; £17,000 to £50,000 (for picture editing) on newspapers.

Qualifications: none required, though some have done some form of degree or diploma. Should have an interest in and some knowledge of photography. Many start as juniors in agencies and then switch to publications.

Will suit you if you: are organised and resourceful; are a fast, unflappable worker, communicative, able to see how pictures will appear in print; have a good eye, visual memory, and knowledge of current affairs.

Perks: the freebies associated with journalism (see FEATURES EDITOR).

Pitfalls: the worry of losing a sheaf of colour transparencies – the charge is around £400 per picture!

Future opportunities: people often switch from agencies, to magazines, to newspapers. Or you can open your own picture library.

How to get in: • careers info from SPREd, Society of Picture Researchers and Editors, BM Box 259, London WC1N 3XX.• apply to picture agencies/libraries (addresses in *The Picture Researcher's Handbook*) • apply to magazines, books, newspapers (addresses in the *Writers' and Artists' Yearbook*) • see job ads in the *Guardian* on Mondays.

'Could you get me some pictures of Paris please,' is the sort of request you don't think much of if you're a picture researcher. It's your role to get more precise knowledge of the art director's requirements. So you try to establish the tone and purpose of the pictures required. If possible, you read the article or chapter these Paris pics are going to illustrate. And then you make a call to the best photo library for the subject, and ask them for *precisely* what you want. Or you might go in and browse through their files. Or, on newspapers, you might commission a photographer.

From now on, everything is highly organised: it has to be, because pictures are flimsy things, easily lost, and valuable. The library books them out in your name, you book them in on your computer or written records.

The art director makes a selection, you return the rejects to the library and, later, follow those with the pics that were used once they're back from the printers. It all sounds very easy, but you could do this with thousands of pictures every week; the potential for confusion is endless: the editor takes them home, loses them in the car and denies all knowledge of them, or you file them in the wrong place . . .

This job demands a high level of ability as well as the knack of getting on with colleagues: you must often track down elusive pictures and get them to the art director within an hour. At the top of a big picture desk, your role becomes managerial. In newspapers, this means going into the morning conference where the day's stories are roughly decided, then setting your team to work . . . it's a never-ending process.

RECORD PRODUCER

Working for: yourself, on contract to record companies and musicians.

Salary range: £20,000 to £50,000+

Qualifications: none required, though increasingly some do have related diplomas and degrees; but the general philosophy seems to be: if you want to do it, get on in there now!

Will suit you if you: are creative, technically minded, resourceful, sociable; have commercial acumen; are motivated – a self-starter.

Perks: being your own boss in a glamorous industry.

Pitfalls: tough to get established; long hours in dark stuffy studios.

Future opportunities: if you manage to make a couple of records and they don't work, you'll probably go back to being a sound engineer; if you succeed, fame and riches follow. You could start up your own recording studio.

How to get in: • consider likely courses: two are run by Department of Performing Arts & Media Studies, Salford College of Technology, Adelphi, Peru Street, Salford M3 6EQ • get a lowly job in a recording studio – once you've co-produced a couple of records try to get a manager who'll help you to win work and negotiate fees (names and addresses for both in *Music Week Directory*) • read *Music Week* for industry info.

You are the one who actually records musicians and singers in the studio, making sure the sound is mixed to produce the desired effect (if you don't have the technical expertise, your engineer will). Nowadays you're almost certainly going to be freelance, hired by A&R MANAGERS at record companies to produce specific records. And to do them, you hire studio space (or maybe have your own studio that you also hire out to others).

It's a technical and creative job, and record producers come from both those backgrounds. Opinion is divided as to which route is best. 'The best record producers begin as artistes then switch,' says one record producer manager, sniffily. But, on the other hand, many successful producers do start as juniors in a recording studio, then work their way up: tea girl/boy, tape operator, assistant engineer . . .

You'll probably rise with the bands you produce records for, so it makes sense to be friendly to everyone at your level: struggling bands, talent scouts, not to mention the A&R managers. The opening could come at any time: a band that hasn't made it yet wants a demo tape; you do it for them and it wins them a contract, and you win more work on the strength of that success.

SET DESIGNER

Working for: theatre companies, mostly freelance paid per production.

Salary range: £1,100 to £2,000, up to £20,000+ per production.

Qualifications: a BA Hons in Theatre Design from a range of colleges (for three good ones see below). You do a foundation course in general Art and Design – quality varies so if in doubt as to which to choose, ask advice from the college you'd like to go on to afterwards. Some designers also do an MA.

Will suit you if you: are creative, imaginative, articulate, practical; have a good eye; manually dextrous; immerse yourself in theatre, reading; can work equally happily on your own or in a team; have a good business sense.

Perks: being your own boss; seeing your own original idea in glorious 3-D on a major West End or Broadway stage; working with the stars.

Pitfalls: irregular income, especially in the early years; having some ingenious part of your set go publicly wrong.

Future opportunities: increasing scope for travel. The ideal is to win the commission to design the set of a major hit, then enjoy royalties for years to come from all countries that copy your original design.

How to get in: • contact The Design Council, 28 Haymarket, London SW1Y 4SU, tel 071–839 8000 • shop around the colleges, including: Central St Martin's College of Art and Design, Southampton Row, London WC1B 4AP, tel 071–753 9090; BIAD, University of Central England, Corporation Street, Birmingham B4 7DX, tel 021–331 5000; Nottingham Trent University, Burton Street, Nottingham, NG1 4BU, tel (0602) 418418.

Set designers are briefed by the director, then generally work on their own at home. They visit the theatre for visual checks, returning to construct a working set model and technical drawings from which the workshops construct the real thing. In many cases, they design the costumes too. Closer to the opening of the production, they're constantly in the theatre, altering costumes as necessary, checking the set and props.

Generally set designers are commissioned on the basis of their reputation. But when you first start, you have no reputation, so you do the most useful thing: you network. At a good college the lecturers will be active designers, and you will have already made a few useful contacts in the industry along with learning technical skills. At the end of your course the college invites directors to view students' work in the annual degree show. Some come, and you do your best to fix up appointments with the ones who didn't, to show them your portfolio.

At first, you'll help established designers on a freelance basis: you might construct a set model, or complete the technical drawings which will be handed to the workshops; or you might even make or buy props. You do anything you're asked, because if you do it well, the next time that designer is too busy to take on a modest project, they may well recommend . . . you.

TV RESEARCHER

Working for: BBC and ITV stations throughout the UK; satellite; cable stations.

Salary range: £11,000 to £25,000

Qualifications: though the ability to get a job and then do it are the only real criteria, you have a better chance of getting in if you have a good degree (subject not important unless you do specialist programmes . . . in business, botany, religion etc.) plus some related experience in print journalism – even the university newspaper.

Will suit you if you: are bright, articulate, a fast worker, resourceful, creative, resilient, competitive and don't give up.

Perks: good opportunities for travel; some free review books; films; music etc. depending on the subject matter of your programmes.

Pitfalls: low job security; can be a back-stabbing business; work pressures often mean you have to cancel social dates at short notice.

Future opportunities: classic route to the role of producer, which has been known to take just fifteen months; move to newspapers or magazines.

How to get in: • BBC Corporate Recruitment Services, 201 Wood Lane, London W12 7TS, tel 081–752 5252, 9 a.m.–5 p.m. • independent TV stations direct • read *The Official ITV Careers Handbook* • see job ads and industry info in *Broadcast*, *Television Week*, *Stage and Television Today*, the *Guardian* on Mondays • apply like mad, and network if you can – many jobs never get advertised so ring producers and 'sell' yourself over the phone.

Behind every coiffed newsreader, every roving presenter, there's a team of researchers who laboured to make that programme possible.

As a researcher, you will work for a particular department or programme – it could be current affairs, a chat show, a nature series (drama has the fewest researchers). On current affairs you find news stories – in practice, a lot of them come to you in the form of press announcements, leaks, and other information from thousands of different sources . . . and you scour the media to keep up to date.

You also find suitable interview subjects, do the interview yourself with a camera team, or arrange for subjects to come into the studio to be quizzed by a presenter. You organise film material, by going out with a camera team, or locating what you need in film archives. And finally you write a script for the presenter (who might rewrite it to suit their style).

When a chat show host has a laid-back conversation with a celebrity, you might be the one who found the celebrity and all but pushed them into the chair. You shortlist likely subjects and put requests through their publicist or agent. More often than not, the ones who say yes are the ones who have a new book/record/something to plug, so you need to know who's producing what. But often, then, their publicists come to you.

SECTION

GREAT OUTDOORS AND TRAVEL

To believe that jobs have to be in offices is to seriously limit your options. There's a whole world out there, bursting with opportunities and these are increasing all the time.

Europe's new single market together with faster, cheaper long-haul flights mean there's never been a better time to get adventurous – whether you're in the holiday business, or you believe flying is most fun when *you're* the pilot, or you enjoy collecting flowers in the jungle.

But you don't *have* to go far to have a good time working out of doors. In Britain, too, there are plenty of opportunities for the free spirit. You could become a manager of hills and woodland, protecting our native wildlife; teach jaded business executives a thing or two about sailing or rock-climbing; become a professional gardener; or build homes.

In this sector, the choices stretch as far as the horizon, and beyond.

AIR STEWARDESS

Working for: airlines.

Salary range: £7,000 to £18,000, plus overseas allowances.

Qualifications: depends on the airline – Virgin says you must be educated to GCSE standard, aged twenty to twenty-eight 5'4"–6'2" tall, with weight in proportion, resident in UK, in good health, hold a valid passport, not wear glasses (contact lenses are fine); nursing, catering or flying experience help. BA requires a language.

Will suit you if you: have a pleasant, reassuring and helpful manner; enjoy irregular hours; can cope in a crisis, and like travel!

Perks: seeing the world; heavily discounted travel for you and your family.

Pitfalls: aircraft air dries out the skin; jet lag; dealing with difficult passengers; missing out on social events at home.

Future opportunities: become a senior cabin crew member; British-trained crews are popular with foreign airlines; move into a managerial role.

How to get in: • contact all airlines, including British Airways plc, Meadowbank, PO Box 59, 680 Bath Road, Hounslow, Middx TW5 9QX • send or phone for info and application form from Virgin Atlantic Airways, 2nd Floor, Ashdown House, High Street, Crawley, West Sussex RH10 1DQ, tel (0293) 562345 8.30 a.m.–6 p.m. • read *Travel Trade Gazette*.

It's no surprise to learn that airlines are bombarded by would-be air stewardesses. The likes of BA and Virgin regularly freeze recruitment for a few months, but don't be deterred – apply again.

The last thing you should say on your application or in the interview is that you want to be a stewardess because you like travel – what they are looking for is personality, combined with commonsense, practical skills and a generally good appearance.

Sarah Sinclair, thirty-two, is a stewardess who works on 747s with Virgin, flying to America and the Far East. She first went to catering college, and worked in the catering and clothing industries before applying to Virgin. 'Those skills come in handy, and probably helped me get this job.'

It pays to shop around to find an airline that suits you. Each airline has something different to offer, though the job itself is similar everywhere. Much of your work is like being a waitress in the air, only with some crucial added responsibilities. You serve meals, drinks, sell duty-free goods, reassure anxious passengers, respond quickly in emergencies.

Be warned: the combination of good times – basking in the sun on a Miami beach on a Monday morning – and bad times – messing up a relationship because you're not there when it matters – can be curiously addictive. Stewardesses find they get hooked on constant travel, feeling bored if they're at home for too long. And later? The choice is to keep on flying, or go into management.

ARCHAEOLOGIST

Working for: museums, local authorities, English Heritage, universities.

Salary range: £6,000 to £25,000.

Qualifications: people can work their way up on digs, in museums, starting as a volunteer if necessary, but most get on by first getting a degree in archaeology. See Council for British Archaeology, below.

Will suit you if you: are actively curious about how people lived in the past; have a detective's instinct for unravelling clues, the patience to reconstruct damaged objects, an organised brain; enjoy digging dirt.

Perks: free travel and lodging; handling treasures; thrilling discoveries.

Pitfalls: generally a low-paid profession; long tedious periods.

Future opportunities: wide-ranging – the past is a growth industry! Most glam job for the experienced: archaeological consultant.

How to get in: • send an A5 SAE for careers and courses info to The Council for British Archaeology, The King's Manor, York YO1 2EP; or ring with specific questions (0904) 433925, 9 a.m.–5.30 p.m. • get in touch directly with organisers of any digs that interest you • see job ads in the *Guardian* on Saturdays • if you fancy getting your feet wet, write for info to The Nautical Archaeological Society, c/o Institute of Archaeology, 31–34 Gordon Square, London WC1H 0PY.

Indiana Jones made digging for buried treasure look rugged, but the reality is far tougher, according to Carol Pyrah, twenty-two, currently vetting planning applications for historic buildings at the Council for British Archaeology. One year after graduating, only 20 per cent of her class have permanent work.

The most common first job is working on a dig as a low-paid junior. A finds assistant on the Sutton Hoo research project, an Anglo Saxon burial mound, for example, earns £120 per week. You catalogue exactly what's been found, and do basic cleaning of bones and pottery with small brushes.

As you get more senior you'll become a finds researcher, writing reports for the project archive, publishing your findings in an academic journal. The latter's important in this career, to build your reputation. With a university degree you are likely to start publishing sooner (Carol is co-writing her first book with an Oxford don), and you build up useful contacts – the professors know where the best jobs are.

There are plenty of areas in which to specialise. One of the most dynamic currently is science in archaeology, in which you analyse human bones and artefacts – the skills you gain are increasingly being used by police forces. Liverpool and Bradford Universities are good places to study this.

Another small but growing branch is archaeological diving. Remember the *Nanking* shipwreck with its cargo of china? Here's a recent job ad plucked from the *Guardian*: 'Archaeological Diver for an Elizabethan wreck off Alderney. Pay £150 a week, with free accommodation and fares.' Indiana Jones would go for it like a shot! And so could you.

THE ARMED FORCES

Working for: RAF, Royal Navy, Army.

Salary range: officers £8,720 to £52,808; £7,139 while at university (including grant); other ranks £7,774 (if 17½+ on entry) to £24,053.

Qualifications: regulars just have to pass an entry test, though in some jobs GCSEs grades A–C are preferred; officers need two A Levels and five GCSEs or be accepted to study for an honours degree (approximately one-third start their Forces career with a degree) and they have a three-day theory and practical test (e.g. crossing a river with a tyre, two mates and a plank) plus interview. All must pass a medical; some jobs require other qualifications; age range at entry is pretty broad – sixteen to thirty-two – but it varies from job to job.

Will suit you if you: are bright and active; show initiative; enjoy organised communal life; are fairly nomadic, and adept at shaping your own career.

Perks: travel; the opportunity to learn a whole range of new skills; generous pensions after retirement at fifty-five; the element of 'what-you-see-is-what-you-get' – there's more promotion by merit and less nepotism than in the civilian sector.

Pitfalls: you're committed to a fixed term of service (you can get out sooner but there may be some financial loss); the rigid hierarchy will not appeal to all; the Armed Forces operate today in a mainly preventive way (stop war before it starts) but there are obvious war-zone dangers.

Future opportunities: there is a highly organised promotional structure, which mostly works (though some areas have promotion freezes). After your services career, your skills will be sought after in the commercial sector.

How to get in: • contact your local Army careers office, Royal Navy careers office, RAF careers office – details in the phone book.

'I always wanted to be a navigator,' say Flight Lieutenant Wendy Smith, twenty-eight, who navigates Hercules transport planes to war zones like Iraq and Sarajevo, as well as to more peaceful spots around the world. 'But when I walked into the careers office at Bournemouth and asked how to apply, the sergeant laughed and said I couldn't do it. So I joined and waited till the policy changed . . . When I qualified, I sent a letter to that same sergeant, who was delighted.'

Today you can do almost anything you want to do in the Armed Forces. There are still restrictions, in the Army especially, but things are changing so rapidly that, like Wendy, you can join and be ready to grab opportunities.

Pilot, navigator, driver, cook, doctor, nurse, physiotherapist, shop manager, oceanographer, weapons engineer and weather forecaster are just some of the careers you can follow within the Forces. The advantage is the security: you get training, accommodation . . . no impoverished student you, eking out a little grant. The disadvantage is that it's highly competitive and difficult to get in, especially as the Forces are being slimmed down. Mental and physical preparation before you even apply is no bad thing.

BILINGUAL SECRETARY

Working for: companies in UK and overseas; Foreign Office; international bodies from EC to UN.

Salary range: £11,000 to £25,000

Qualifications: sound secretarial skills – 50 wpm typing, 90 wpm shorthand. There's a whole range of secretarial courses with languages on offer, but longer ones of one to two years, run by local colleges and administered by bodies such as City and Guilds or the London Chamber of Commerce and Industry are better received by employers than crash courses. A GCSE or A Level in your chosen language is usually required to get on your course, and by the end of it you should understand how the relevant country operates in business and economic terms. Make sure your college provides up-to-date teaching on word-processors and current business methods.

Perks: the kudos of foreign language skills; some travel.

Pitfalls: hours often longer than nine-to-five; you really work for that salary.

Future opportunities: free trade from 1993 between European countries, plus business links with Japan and Middle East mean that this is a growth area.

How to get in: • ask your local careers officer (in the phone book under your borough's services) or local colleges for info on secretarial courses with language skills • write for info on (internationally respected) courses to The London Chamber of Commerce and Industry Examinations Board, Marlowe House, Station Road, Sidcup, Kent DA15 7BJ • write to The Institute of Linguists, 24a Highbury Grove, London N5 2EA for their publications list of careers booklets • for jobs, contact recruitment agency Bilinguasec, 49 Maddox Street, London W1R 9LA, tel 071–493 6446; write directly to any organisations you'd like to work for • see job ads in the national quality papers.

As a bilingual secretary you could work for the sales director of a company exporting clothing or computers to Europe and beyond. Say your language is French: it'll be up to you to chase by phone – in fluent, persuasive French – that store in Paris which has yet to pay for a recent order. You'll also receive dictation in English to type up in French. You'll set up meetings with companies abroad . . . and as your career progresses you'll probably be the one negotiating deals.

Or you could get a secretarial job in a British embassy abroad; or work for an aid organisation in Africa. As French is the language most of us learn, there's a tactical advantage in learning one of the languages most others *don't* know, such as Arabic, Japanese, or Russian. But you must have a liking for the relevant country.

For the best jobs, good secretarial and language qualifications matter – as does a knowledge of how business is *really* done in the relevant country. 'To earn good money as a bilingual secretary you need to know all the short cuts of your country,' explains one recruitment expert. Get in the know by doing work experience in the country of your choice.

BOTANIST/PLANT COLLECTOR

Working for: botanical gardens and other plant research establishments; pharmaceutical, cosmetics and agricultural businesses.

Salary range: £9,500 to £40,000.

Qualifications: best route is through a degree in botany followed by a Masters or a PhD. Oxford, Reading, Cambridge, Leicester, Manchester and Strathclyde universities are all good. Or start as a school-leaver and train for a diploma as you work (Kew runs its own courses). 'Ability is more important than qualifications,' says one personnel officer. But plant collectors do tend to have academic backgrounds. HORTI-CULTURALISTS also collect plants.

Will suit you if you: have a scientific interest in how plants work; care for the environment; are methodical, thorough; and an intrepid traveller.

Perks: you're doing something for the environment; free plants; fresh air; unusual travel; you could identify a new cereal crop to stop famine in the Third World . . .

Pitfalls: from the Amazon to Zimbabwe, the risk of tropical diseases.

Future opportunities: interest in things green is blooming, and so are openings in the commercial sector, not to mention specialist journalistic jobs in TV and the press. Be the next David Bellamy, or perhaps an environmental archaeologist, analysing plants from the past.

How to get in: • write to the personnel depts of botanical gardens: The Royal Botanical Gardens, Edinburgh, 20a Inverleith Row, Edinburgh EH3 5LR; The Royal Botanic Gardens, Kew, Richmond, Surrey TW9 3AB; ask your library for other addresses • careers info from Wiltshire Guidance Services, County Careers Centre, County Hall Annex, Bythesea Road, Trowbridge BA14 8EZ • see job ads in *New Scientist*, *Nature*, national and local press.

Mondays can be hell – but not if you're a plant collector with a yen for travel. You could be in Borneo, on a special trip to gather samples of little-known species of hollies to transport back to the herbarium (plant archives) at your botanical garden. You have your hands full gathering seeds, snipping branches, putting them into a flower press and carefully cataloguing everything, but there are local bearers to lead you through the forest, carry provisions, set up camp and cook. At night, exhausted, you sleep under tarpaulin stretched over bamboo canes.

'It's not all travel, though,' says Susan Andrews, who specialises in hollies at Kew. 'We can spend up to a year getting permission from the authorities of the country we plan to visit – there's plenty of letter writing.' Between trips, you'll spend long hours examining the plant specimens, working out where a newly discovered plant fits in the scheme of things and what useful chemical properties it may have.

People within this little publicised career say it's not too difficult to get in whatever stage you're at. But since it's essentially about academic study, degrees are valuable, as is a bit of unpaid work experience.

CHARTERED SURVEYOR

Working for: private practices, estate agencies, central and local government, property developers and industrial companies.

Salary range: £6,000 to £7,000 during a two-year probationary period (unpaid for some unlucky ones today) to anything up to £250,000!

Qualifications: you'll do a degree course in chartered surveying (there are approximately seventy-five courses in the UK – see below). Reading University is good. Or join a firm of surveyors direct and train on day release at a local college. People with an unrelated degree can do a conversion course.

Will suit you if you: are a problem-solver, analytical; can handle figures; are an effective communicator; care for the environment.

Perks: a car; you'll never buy an unsound property!

Pitfalls: your career largely depends on the state of the property market – flat in recent years; you'll visit sites in all weathers.

Future opportunities: once you are qualified and have gained experience, you could become wealthy as the partner of a large practice, acting as a consultant to developers and business owners.

How to get in: • careers and accredited courses info from The Royal Institution of Chartered Surveyors, 12 Great George Street, Parliament Square, London SW1P 3AD, tel 071–222 7000, 9 a.m.–5.30 p.m.

Chartered surveyors end up in a bewildering range of occupations but their basic role is to turn building projects into reality then keep them in good order. That includes doing surveys on the houses the rest of us want to buy, to ensure they're sound. 'I like the fact that I can look at any building and understand why it is made that way,' says Diane, twenty-five.

During your training you will have discovered a huge choice of tempting career directions. You could become a minerals surveyor, finding out through soil analysis and other means the amount of oil, zinc, or other minerals to be found in a particular site, having it mined, then putting the landscape back into order again when the miners have left. You could go into estate management, looking after a lord's acres, or an environmental charity. But the majority choose property development.

In a residential property practice, you visit homes to do surveys, making a visual search for bad signs like a leaking roof or damp basement, then write a report. You also supervise improvements to a property. If you are working directly for a developer, you do a survey of housing requirements in an area, put together a proposal for planning permission, and present it to the local planning department.

In your twenties you'd expect to get £17,500 to £25,000 in a residential property practice, or working for a developer. A few years ago it was more. 'The market is flat,' says one recruitment consultant. But he adds that once you get the all-important letters ARICS (Associate of the Royal Institution of Chartered Surveyors) after your name, two years after completing your degree, your earning potential becomes immense.

COUNTRYSIDE RANGER

Working for: local authorities, national parks, Forestry Commission, private estates, Crown estate, National Trust, English Heritage and other land-owning conservation bodies.

Salary range: £8,000 to £15,000

Qualifications: no formal ones required, but you should demonstrate an active interest in and knowledge of the countryside. Evidence of voluntary or casual work definitely helps. Some rangers have a degree (in any subject, including environmental subjects, zoology). School-leavers are generally considered too young – you're likely to be twenty-one plus.

Perks: effectively being your own boss; fresh air, getting close to wildlife; some jobs offer free or subsidised accommodation.

Pitfalls: long, irregular hours – your busy times are other people's holidays; you could be up during the night if there are poaching problems, or a local motorbike gang is roaring through the forest.

How to get in: • apply to countryside organisations • for careers info send a large SAE to The Association of Countryside Rangers, Yarrow Lodge, Yarner Wood, Bovey Tracey, Devon TQ13 9LJ.• send A5 SAE to The Environment Council, 14a–21 Elizabeth Street, London SW1, tel 071–278 4736 • see job ads in the national quality papers • read *British Wildlife* (a quarterly) for info – in some libraries, or on subscription from British Wildlife Publishing, tel (0256) 760663.

You are one of the few people in Britain who can wake up in the morning, look out on to forests, lakes and mountains, and say to yourself, 'All this is mine – at least while I'm holding down the job.'

Countryside rangers don't earn very much for their often physical labours, but they say there is an enormous satisfaction in thoroughly getting to know a piece of countryside, through different seasons, and feeling part of it. You will spend at least half your time on the land, mending fences, maintaining paths, monitoring birds and deer.

You will also be managing other staff, and much of the rest of the time you will be dealing with the public. Today, there's a real emphasis on giving people access to, and understanding of, the British countryside. So you provide information boards and leaflets, and talk to the crowds of interested visitors who come at bank holidays and weekends.

Viv Phillips has had several jobs as a ranger, including one in the Seychelles, where she and her husband were rangers together – you regularly find such double posts on offer to couples. Today, she is reserve manager at the ARC Wildfowl Centre near Milton Keynes. 'I'd say it's almost essential to do voluntary work; an awful lot of people are moving into countryside management, and the more practical experience you have, the better. Becoming an active member of one or two societies related to your particular interest, plants, birds etc., is also a good idea.'

CRUISE SHIP STAFF

Working for: cruise shipping lines worldwide: P&O, Cunard, etc.

Salary range: $2,000 to $5,000 per month including tips (most ships pay in US dollars).

Qualifications: cruise ships favour those with vocational qualifications and two years' good experience before going on board: e.g. CATERERS will have done a City and Guilds or similar course and will have done time at a quality hotel or restaurant. Some 'sweat shop' ships don't ask for this (see below).

Will suit you if you: are independent but can work as part of a team in close confines; are flexible and open to cultural differences; have good inner resources; are even-tempered with a pleasant personality.

Perks: travel, travel, travel! Tips galore; tax-free income.

Pitfalls: Cruise lines vary in reputation. Broadly, the European ones treat you well, but watch out for danger signs out of Europe: if a company expects you to pay for your air fare out to the ship, they may expect you to work as a galley slave once you're on board. (But even then you can earn very good tips.)

Future opportunities: for the hotel and entertainment staff, it's not generally seen as a career for life. On dry land again, you'll find in your industry that you're fitter and more able than many landlubbers.

How to get in: • contact cruise ship companies direct: e.g. Fleet Personnel Dept, P&O Cruises Fleet Services Ltd, Dukes Keep, Marsh Lane, Southampton SO9 4GU • for ship hotel posts, write to Supersearch International, Shakespeare House, Shakespeare Street, Newcastle upon Tyne, NE1 6AQ • for hair stylists' posts: Coiffeur Transocean (Overseas) Ltd, Swiss Cottage House, 8–13 Swiss Terrace, London NW6 4RR • for photographers' posts: Cruiseship Picture Company, 132 High Street, Esher, Surrey KT10 9QJ.

Honolulu, Acapulco, Rio de Janeiro and the Seychelles . . . if you work on a cruise ship, these could become more familiar to you than the sights back home.

Cruise ships can be viewed as mobile luxury hotels, with all the facilities and luxuries that a hotel's wealthy clientele would expect. This means you could get a job working as cabin staff, or cooking or waiting in the restaurants, or serving cocktails behind the bar. If your interests are sporty and you have the right qualifications/experience to match, you could run the ship's gym, or be a swimming pool attendant, or take fitness classes on the deck. There's also work to be done in the ships' shops, in hair salons and the casinos, and an ongoing need for entertainers.

Medical staff, secretaries and office workers of every description can find related work on a ship. And – of course – there are openings for ships' crew, the ones who actually run the ship. See MERCHANT NAVY for details of those jobs.

Because there's nowhere to run when you're on a ship, it's more important than it is in most other career to stay friendly with your colleagues, not to mention the passengers in your care who may give you fat tips at the end of their trip. Large companies like P&O encourage social activities for their crews, such as friendly sports matches against local opposition in port.

DIPLOMAT

Working for: the Foreign & Commonwealth Office.

Salary range: start at £7,607/£9,930/£13,869+, depending on your grade, then up to £84,250 plus overseas allowances for you and your family.

Qualifications: you need a minimum of five GCSEs, or equivalent for the lower grade; or two A Levels for a higher grade; most entrants have good degrees from a whole range of subjects, including languages, history, economics, international relations, sciences . . . To enter at the highest grade you'll certainly need a degree. Mature entrants with work experience are also welcomed. You don't need foreign languages, but you'll have to do a language aptitude test.

Will suit you if you: are bright, practical, adventurous and outgoing; have integrity; are independent, adaptable, mature; are able to get on well with a wide range of people; are willing to live and work anywhere in the world.

Perks: travel, travel, travel! You change jobs and countries every three years.

Pitfalls: your partner has to be willing to go wherever you're posted; the highly organised hierarchy won't suit everyone.

Future opportunities: promotion depends on your performance; you learn new skills such as languages and the whole diplomatic experience makes you desirable as a manager in the commercial sector . . . Or you can stay a diplomat and become an ambassador!

How to get in: • get careers info, or arrange a visit to the FCO, by writing or phoning: Recruitment Section, Personnel Policy Department, Foreign & Commonwealth Office, 3 Central Buildings, Matthew Parker Street, London SW1H 9NL, tel 071–210 8121.
• application form from Recruitment and Assessment Services, Alencon Link, Basingstoke, Hants RG21 1JB, tel (0256) 29222.

'You could do it the hard way and work in the same office in Britain day after day and have two weeks abroad every year. Or you could join the Diplomatic Service,' says the Foreign Office, not beating about the bush.

You start in London then have regular postings abroad, training as you need to, being posted back to London from time to time.

One job might see you in an East African country, where you help with aid projects and encourage private investment in the region. You hold meetings with British and local business people to push forward a new scheme to train young people in businesses; you liaise with relief and development organisations to arrange for British aid – funds, food and expertise – to reach the right places.

Another job might find you in the immigration section of the embassy in Islamabad, helping applicants with queries, processing their forms, issuing visas. Yet another might find you providing information where necessary for UK ministers at a conference in Moscow, New York, Milan or Tokyo . . . And your next job will be entirely different: because as an FCO all-rounder, you change not only the country each time, but the department too.

EXPEDITION/TREK LEADER

Working for: adventure tour operators.

Salary range: from nothing (expenses only) to £160 per week (less for drivers).

Qualifications: no formal ones required, though there are lots of graduates in this sector. Must be able to mend broken vehicles – no AA men in the jungle. If driving trucks, will obviously need an appropriate licence. Must demonstrate resourcefulness, initiative, leadership, maturity, and budget-control. An unusual language such as Thai/Mandarin an advantage. For vehicle insurance purposes, you'll probably have to be twenty-five plus.

Will suit you if you: love adventure; are fit, level-headed, a good communicator, efficient organiser/manager, a problem-solver, practical, and flexible.

Perks: working in the most stunning, unspoilt parts of the world. Free travel, board and lodging (in tents and budget hotels).

Pitfalls: low pay, seasonal work, not a long-term career; potential for tropical diseases and injuries.

Future opportunities: adventure holidays are on the up; run your own.

How to get in: • contact all the adventure tour operators such as Exodus, Sherpa – addresses from their ads in walking magazines.

'One night I heard a strange sound coming from the porters' tents. I went to investigate and found they were sharpening their knives. I asked them what they were doing. They explained they had a feud with the young men of the village we would reach tomorrow. They were preparing for a fight. So I told them I'd fire them unless they behaved.'

That account from a trek leader in the Himalayas demonstrates just one of the management skills you'll need to lead an adventure holiday successfully. In a manner of speaking, your expedition is an office on the move, and you're the one in charge. You often have a team of local porters or bearers to cook, carry and set up tents; guides; and, of course, a group of six or ten holiday-makers. All must be kept in line, while giving the holiday-makers the time of their lives. The porters probably won't speak English, though the guides often do.

Some expeditions involve travelling by truck, others by foot (trekking). Truck leaders travel in twos. You need good diagnostic skills to sort out mechanical problems, though companies like Exodus will train you for a few weeks in their workshops if you can demonstrate an affinity for the subject.

Vacancies with all tour operators occur sporadically, so apply to, and get information from, all that appeal to you. Requirements vary: some say no previous experience required. Others want evidence of related experience. But attitude/personality is the clincher.

FOREIGN CORRESPONDENT

Working for: news wire agencies, newspapers, TV and radio.

Salary range: from £15,000 to £50,000+.

Qualifications: variable. Most are graduates, though subject not important. Reuters, one of the biggest world new wire agencies, takes a handful of graduates a year, plus people with business journalism experience. Anyone can choose to move abroad and operate as a 'stringer' i.e., a freelance writer producing news stories and articles for a range of British publications and radio . . . but you need to know your stuff, preferably, having first worked as a staff reporter. Fewer openings on newspapers: start as a trainee reporter, then work up.

Will suit you if you: are inquisitive, linguistic, resourceful, flexible, good at gaining people's confidence, a fluent writer; tireless researcher, fast.

Perks: travel; living expenses; some free plane flights to and fro; with agencies like Reuters, a company flat.

Pitfalls: correspondents may go to the world's most dangerous places; relationships back home can suffer; long, irregular hours.

Future opportunities: what you make of them – but the experience of working abroad tends to make you fit for anything back at home.

How to get in: • contact the National Council for the Training of Journalists, Latton Bush Centre, Southern Way, Harlow, Essex CM18 7BL, tel (0279) 430009 • contact news agencies and newspapers direct – addresses in the *Writers' and Artists' Yearbook* • TV: see TV RESEARCHER • job ads in the *Guardian* and *UK Press Gazette* • read, listen to, watch, all the foreign news you can.

Skim the papers and you'll see just who the foreign correspondents are today. At the bottom of a story about war in Angola, or new millionaires in China, the light italicised letters AP or Reuter appear. Newspapers can't afford to keep staff reporters dotted around the world, so they buy news from the wire agencies who send it in a continuous stream by computer directly into the newspapers' offices.

There are openings on the newspapers. Typically, a paper will send out one or two of its London staff to cover major events, and they do also employ permanent outposts in the major cities like Paris and New York.

But the growth area is strictly electronic. Jo, thirty-two, works for a business wire service in Milan. 'We have to get big news out really fast, because we're in competition with other news services. That can mean writing a story and sending it out just thirty seconds after I got the information.'

Working for a wire service you ring analysts, economists and others in financial institutions to find out what's happening in a particular market, then tap a quick, sharp article into your computer which instantly gets transmitted to newspapers worldwide. Note: a few agencies will let you do work experience in their offices abroad. Ring agency head offices and ask.

HORTICULTURALIST/ LANDSCAPE ARCHITECT

Working for: botanical and private gardens; town parks, market gardens, nurseries, garden centres, landscape contractors; or your own business.

Salary range: £6,000 (less as a trainee) to £20,000+.

Qualifications: Pick your own. You can apply direct to an employer from the age of sixteen onwards, as a YT, training on the job or by block release at a local college; a two- or three-year diploma, a degree or even a Masters, if you plan to go into research. Landscape architects have to gain a degree in the subject, or a similar one, followed by two years' practical experience before qualifying with the Landscape Institute. See addresses below.

Will suit you if you: like an outdoor life, growing things; are patient, fit; can work on your own or with a team; have business sense.

Perks: free plants, healthy lifestyle.

Pitfalls: often low pay; you could be weeding in the rain.

Future opportunities: this industry is blooming. Horticulturalists (professional gardeners) trained in the UK are always in demand at home and abroad, says the Institute of Horticulture. Good opportunities in garden centres where you might rise into management. There are over 2,000 centres in the UK; altogether they employ 30,000 people. Or you can go on to become a gardening correspondent on TV, radio, or in print.

How to get in: • send A5 SAE for careers and courses info to The Institute of Horticulture, PO Box 313, 80 Vincent Square, London SW1P 2PE; or phone 071–976 5951 with specific questions and ask for IoH Secretary • info and courses details for would-be landscape architects from The Landscape Institute, 6/7 Barnard Mews, London SW11 1QU.

We're a nation of gardeners: gardens, parks, fruit bowls, vegetable racks and store cupboards are filled by horticulturalists.

Horticulturalists work in a sensual world – you could be in a herb nursery, sowing basil, thyme, rosemary and marjoram which will end up dried in jars or tied in fresh sprigs, on a supermarket shelf. Or you could be taking scented lavender cuttings to grow then sell in a garden centre. Or pruning apple trees, or weeding asparagus beds . . .

But there are, as you'd expect, some bugs in this career. Work is frantic at harvest time, while employees may be laid off during the winter months. Call on a garden centre or nursery locally, and ask if you can do a few days' unpaid work, to get a feel for whether it would suit you.

Though it's more usual to train, you can choose your own way in. Anna, thirty, is a landscape gardener who began training as an architect, then simply applied architectural skills to her love of gardening. Like her, you could design things as simple as a window box, from £80 a go – or whole garden schemes for private clients.

3

MARINE BIOLOGIST

Working for: voluntary conservation groups and Government-funded bodies such as English Nature, Natural Environment Research Council.

Salary range: £10,000 to £25,000 (most are on £14,000 to £18,000).

Qualifications: a good degree, maybe also an MSc or PhD in marine biology or a similar subject – universities include Southampton, Bangor, Aberystwyth; or you can take on a support role with a BTEC diploma, or A Levels or equivalent. Optional extra: become an advanced diver at a local club (see below).

Will suit you if you: have a strong interest in conservation and the sea, a lively, enquiring mind; are patient, methodical, accurate, and adventurous.

Perks: part of your job could involve diving, and certainly walking in Britain's most beautiful coastal spots; helping to save threatened species.

Pitfalls: you may be out in all weathers.

Future opportunities: the voluntary sector is the biggest growth area; you could work abroad in temperate or tropical seas.

How to get in: • careers info from Plymouth Marine Laboratory, Citadel Hill, Plymouth PL1 2PB • also from Natural Environment Research Council, Polaris House, North Star Avenue, Swindon, Wilts SN2 1EU • learn to dive with the British Sub-Aqua Club – details of your nearest club from BSAC, Telfords Quay, Ellesmere Port, South Wirral, Cheshire L65 4FY, tel 051–357 1951, 9 a.m.–5 p.m.

Imagine this: you're 20 metres under water, off the north-east coast of England. As you hover over sea urchins and starfish, you're writing in shorthand with a chinagraph pencil on a plastic slate – not in shorthand a secretary would recognise, but a marine version, which enables you to record according to an abundance scale the amount and types of sand and sea creatures you find. You and your colleague (as a safety precaution you always dive in twos) also carry collecting bags, to pick up samples and, sometimes, an underwater camera to record changes in regularly visited sites . . .

Marine biologists survey estuaries and coastal waters to discover the effects of pollution and other factors on our marine environment. You certainly don't have to scuba-dive to be a marine biologist, but it's a pleasurable option. However, much of the work takes place in laboratories, analysing, for example, pollutants in marine animals and plants.

It's a job for the naturally curious, the sort who wants to know what makes a mud shrimp build its burrows, whether plankton population growth contributes to global warming, precisely what effect toxic dumping has on oysters and mussels . . . Seventy per cent of our world is covered in water, and so far we've only skimmed the surface in terms of understanding and harnessing its powers. So as a marine biologist, in virtually everything you do, you'll be a pioneer.

MERCHANT NAVY DECK OFFICER

Working for: shipping companies, both cargo and cruise.

Salary range: often on YTS while training, £35 per week; junior officers £12,000 to £15,000; ship's master (captain) £50,000.

Qualifications: these vary, so ask individual companies, but usually four or five GCSEs grades A–C including English, maths and physics; or two good A Levels including maths or physics. You also have to pass a medical.

Will suit you if you: are a good team-worker, practical, tolerant, self-sufficient; have good inner resources to withstand long periods of boredom.

Perks: free travel to countless countries.

Pitfalls: you can't leave work and colleagues behind at the end of your day.

Future opportunities: Britain's fleet is much smaller than it used to be so openings are fairly limited; you can also work on boats from other countries (but watch out for sweat shops – see CRUISE SHIP STAFF), rise to the rank of ship's master, or change careers completely back on land.

How to get in: • careers info and details of shipping companies from The Chamber of Shipping, 2–5 Minories, London EC3N 1BJ, tel 071–702 1100 • The National Union of Marine, .Aviation and Shipping Transport Officers can give advice: UMAST, 750–760 High Road, London E11 3BB, tel 081–989 6677.

The ideal is to be accepted by a major shipping company such as Cunard or P&O, then train up while employed by them: they sponsor you through naval college. Otherwise, you have to fund part or all of your training, and then apply to shipping companies for each sea voyage you make.

As a deck officer, your work includes navigating the ship, managing crew, supervising loading and unloading of cargo (or passengers). During your training, as a deck cadet, you spend periods at sea and periods at college, studying for an HND in nautical science.

Alternative careers you might equally follow include those of engineer, learning how to run the ship's engines; purser/catering officer, in charge of all provisions and cooking; radio officer; and pre-trained medical staff, chiefly nurses and doctors.

Though ships have become more modern (slightly roomier cabins) and the management hierarchy is well-structured, there's a lot of room for bedlam on a ship containing people of several different nationalities who see nothing but sea for weeks. So you have to be strong on survival skills and have the knack of getting on with colleagues you don't always naturally like. By the time you've learnt those tricks, you'll be more than a match for any landlubber workplaces when you finally settle back on dry land.

OUTDOOR ACTIVITIES INSTRUCTOR

Working for: outdoor activity centres for LEAs and private companies.

Salary range: £50 to £140 per day for instructor certificate holders.

Qualifications: usually aged twenty-four plus. Must show proof of technical outdoor skills such as rock-climbing, canoeing, sailing, acquired through short courses and adventure holidays. 'The more such qualifications you have, the more likely you are to get on,' says one employer.

Will suit you if you: can lead and motivate people; are fit and responsible.

Perks: free or subsidised food and accommodation; working in stunning parts of Britain; you'll reach optimum levels of fitness and courage.

Pitfalls: falling off a mountain; dealing with the odd difficult student; you'll be out in all weathers.

Future opportunities: it's a small industry (Outward Bound employs approximately 250 people in the UK), but a growing one; good instructors are often head-hunted. Start your own local walking/canoeing business.

How to get in: • contact The Sports Council, 16 Woburn Place, London WC1H 0QP, tel 071–388 1277, 9 a.m.–5 p.m. • instructor certificate courses at Plas y Brenin, The National Mountain Centre, Capel Curig, Gwynedd LL24 0ET, tel (06904) 214 • contact the Outward Bound Trust, Chestnut Field, Regent Place, Rugby CV21 2PJ • write to the principals at activity centres (large SAEs to all of the above).

Would-be outdoor activity instructors must demonstrate 'an ability to initiate and structure their own life experiences, from climbing major peaks to working in cities,' says the Outward Bound Trust.

That sums up what these activities are about. Face up to your fears of climbing a mountain, and you can face up to boardroom battles too. But, as an instructor, the mountains and lakes of Britain *are* your office. At 9 a.m. on a typical Monday morning, you might be abseiling down a sheer mountain drop in Wales, looking after not only yourself, but perhaps ten others who could be school children, private individuals, or executives.

'Sometimes I can't believe I'm lucky enough to be paid to do this,' says one instructor in her mid-twenties. What is for other people a quick break away from humdrum reality, is to you, as an instructor, a way of life. This does sometimes mean getting up before dawn to reach a particular white water canoeing site, or kipping in a sleeping bag under the night stars.

You can do short mountain (and other) instructor courses at Plas y Brenin. To get a job at the centre, you also have to show that you have the personal qualities of resourcefulness, initiative, kindness and stamina – a 20-mile hike one day, rock-climbing the next, could wipe out a lesser person. You don't have to know it all from the start though. As you work you'll be taught other skills to the level required to teach them to others. Soon you should be able to take groups hill-walking, navigating, climbing, caving . . . You'll be an adventurous all-rounder.

PILOT

Working for: airlines, air charter firms, air taxi companies.

Salary range: when qualified, from £25,000 to £45,000+

Qualifications: you'll need a commercial pilot's licence from the Civil Aviation Authority; there are several grades from flying light aircraft to large commercial aircraft. To go to flying school (approximately one year, and very expensive) apply direct to airline companies for sponsorship. You usually need two A Levels and five GCSEs grades A–C including English, maths and a science. BA operates a cadet pilot training scheme.

Will suit you if you: are generally fit with good eyesight (glasses can be worn for some sight correction); are calm, confident; can cope in emergencies; can stay alert through long patches of routine; are quick-thinking, a good communicator; work well in a team but can make your own decisions; have leadership qualities.

Perks: travel and the thrill of flying.

Pitfalls: the stress of being responsible for hundreds of passengers and an expensive plane; relationships can suffer.

Future opportunities: once qualified, there are plenty of employers. You can switch airlines; you can move into management or pilot training; run your own flying school or air-taxi service, flying bigwigs across the country.

How to get in: career and courses info from Civil Aviation Authority, CAA House, 45–59 Kingsway, London WC2B 6TE, tel 071–379 7311, 9 a.m.–5 p.m. • industry info in *Flight International* • contact airlines direct for sponsored training – including BA, the biggest (British Airways plc, Meadowbank, PO Box 59, 680 Bath Road, Hounslow, Middx TW5 9QX).

Training to be a pilot used to be done with the student sitting, unharnessed, on the wing of the plane while he watched the pilot fly the plane and tried to pick up tips.

Today, it's infinitely more complex, and more expensive, but you can still get there if you're determined. It's notoriously hard to get airlines, even BA, to pay for the full commercial training. Apply to all of them as persuasively as you can (recruitment staff at BA have said in the past they would welcome more women applicants).

Failing that, people have been known to remortgage their houses to go to flying school, but a more popular method is to learn the 'self-improvement' way: train for a private pilot's licence with a local flying club (about £4,000), then build up to 700 hours and qualify for a full Commercial Pilot's Licence.

At that point you can make a living as a company pilot, or be a co-pilot with some of the smaller airlines. If you still fancy yourself at the controls of a 747, there's another licence, the Airline Transport Pilot's Licence to be studied and struggled for. See also ARMED FORCES.

RELIEF/DEVELOPMENT WORKER

Working for: aid groups such as Save the Children, United Nations, VSO.

Salary range: VSO employees abroad earn from £9,500 to £18,500; volunteers get local rates only; in head office £10,500–£30,000. The UN are the fat cats of aid work: one thirty-year-old's salary after tax was quoted as £30,000.

Qualifications: you need a proven skill: nursing, midwifery, agricultural economics, engineering, financial management etc. City and Guilds, degree or vocational qualifications. Top UN jobs require a Masters degree.

Will suit you if you: are flexible, resourceful, tolerant, and keen to help others.

Perks: travel; overseas salary tax-free or at less tax than in the UK; subsidised accommodation; free flights there and back.

Pitfalls: scale of the problems can be depressing; obvious dangers in a war zone; potential for tropical diseases.

Future opportunities: once you're in, there are plenty of new posts to go for – including admin. jobs back in Britain for people tired of the field.

How to get in: send A4 SAE to VSO at 317 Putney Bridge, London SW15 2PN, tel 081–780 1331 • send A4 SAE to Save the Children, 17 Grove Lane, London SE5 8RD, tel 071–703 5400 9–5 p.m. • send A5 SAE to UN Information Centre, 20 Buckingham Gate, London SW1E 6LB, tel 071–630 1981 • see job ads in the *Guardian* on Saturdays.

Anywhere that's war-torn, bereft of food, crowded with refugees . . . these are the places for you as a relief and development worker. Relief work involves offering emergency assistance such as food and drugs; development is where you teach local people your own skills – medical, engineering or whatever – so that they can continue helping their community after you've gone. Useful skills for development workers include accountancy, editing, computer programming, dress-making, building . . . almost anything.

Apply to agencies who could offer a posting, perhaps to Somalia, Ethiopia, Sudan or Nepal. Claire Marrack has spent six months to two years in each of those countries with Save the Children. She's qualified as a nurse, midwife and health visitor. When she originally applied, the charity had no vacancies, but as famine swept Sudan and Ethiopia, they rang back and said, 'Can you go?' She went.

As a nurse or doctor, your job is to provide basic medical services, running a cottage hospital, training local staff. The scale of the problems can be overwhelming. But workers say it's a wonderful feeling when you've passed on techniques that will carry on saving lives.

Accommodation ranges from the palatial to mud huts. Working hours are long, social amenities basic. Relief workers reckon it's a good idea to work in Britain between postings, to unwind, and for the cv – strangely, some UK employers sometimes think work abroad is not proper work.

RESORT MANAGER

Working for: tour operator companies of all sizes (biggest is Thomson, who own Thomson Holidays, Skytours, Horizon and Wings).

Salary range: reps from around £250 per month plus allowances; a resort manager gets around £10,000 per annum plus allowances.

Qualifications: no formal qualifications generally required but you must be fluent in English plus at least one other language. Thomson also has a graduate entry scheme. Some firms specify a minimum age of twenty-one.

Will suit you if you: can handle difficult customers, crises and the unexpected; are cheerful and confident; can make decisions and be responsible.

Perks: holiday concessions, plus a commission when you arrange excursions.

Pitfalls: low pay; it could be just seasonal work initially; you may face being stranded abroad with 300 panicking holiday-makers if your company folds!

Future opportunities: many go into management in their head offices or into other branches of the tourist industry.

How to get in: • application form and job details from the Personnel Dept, Thomson Tour Operations, Greater London House, Hampstead Road, London NW1, tel 071-387 9321 • write direct to other operators of your choice – pluck their names from holiday brochures, or the travel pages of weekend papers • see job ads and inside info in *Travel Trade Gazette* • contact ABTA National Training Board, Waterloo House, 11–17 Chertsey Road, Woking, Surrey GU21 5AL.

The pay isn't great, but when the sun's out, and your board and lodging is either free or subsidised, things are looking up! Salaries improve as your career progresses, from rep through senior rep, head rep, to resort manager. And since tourism is a growing industry, there are real opportunities abroad and in Britain.

At first, you'll be based in a resort, in Greece, Italy, Spain, France, the Canaries, Tunisia, Barbados . . . or any one of countless other countries. During the season you switch resorts, even countries, as required. Your job will be to greet holiday-makers at the airport when they arrive, take them in a coach to their hotel, give them a welcome talk and a drinks party; be on hand to answer their queries, arrange special excursions, and deal with emergencies as they arise – you'll find that holiday-makers regularly lose their passports, their money, get drunk or get lost!

It's up to you to make their stay as pleasant and as problem-free as possible. That includes keeping a cool head in real crises, such as when you need to arrange – in a foreign language – medical treatment or emergency flights home for holiday-makers who are taken ill.

As a rep or resort manager you work hard as you are on call to deal with any problems night and day . . . but the climate is nearly always balmy, and you do get wonderful opportunities to travel.

RIDING INSTRUCTOR

Working for: riding schools, centres, stables; activity holiday centres.

Salary range: £6,000 to £15,000. You may be paid (perhaps on YTS), or get nothing, or even have to pay, during your initial training on the job.

Qualifications: employment prospects are better with qualifications (you may need some GCSEs for these: you train for three tiers of British Horse Society examinations, usually while working but some go to a large training centre then get a job). It can take a week or six months to get qualified, depending on your previous riding skills.

Will suit you if you: love horses and the way of life associated with stables; are healthy and strong; are happy to muck in and muck out; have a reassuring, responsible, friendly manner.

Perks: you can combine instructing with competing: get a name for yourself, and you'll become more sought after as an instructor.

Pitfalls: your small salary could be even smaller if you enjoy any 'extras': live-in accommodation, further training, or stabling for your own horse.

Future opportunities: there is work all around the country, most of which is not well paid. You could start your own stables; become an equestrian writer.

How to get in: • send £1 for career pack to The British Horse Society, British Equestrian Centre, Stoneleigh, Kenilworth, Warwicks CV8 2LR, tel (0203) 696697, 9 a.m.–5 p.m. • working pupil situations in *Horse and Hound*.

You lead a string of horses and riders through a pretty Irish mountain pass on a clear spring day. Or, you give a group of handicapped children their first lesson on a horse – the thrilled looks on their faces is wonderful to watch. Or, you preside over a competition and help to judge the winners. Or, you're riding in the competition and you *are* one of the winners . . .

Then again, more often than not, you're shovelling mucky straw out of a stable and replacing it with new. You're exhausted and you've got six more stalls to do after this. Being a riding instructor is a mixture of pleasurable exercise in beautiful surroundings, and back-breaking work.

This career, especially in its early stages, is a labour of love. The commonest way of starting is to become a working pupil at one of the larger centres, and receive tuition in exchange for your work. Employers say pupils are more likely to be accepted if their enthusiasm and ability come across; if you've done casual work with animals before, so much the better. The training, whether you do it by this route, or by going to one of the large training centres, or to a local college with time spent at a stable when not studying, is extremely practical: it's teaching you how to do your job right down to cleaning tackle and to cleaning up horse manure.

You're unlikely to become a millionaire. But instructors say the job satisfaction is high.

SALES EXECUTIVE COMMERCIAL AIRLINES

Working for: airline companies such as BA, KLM, Lufthansa, TWA, Virgin.

Salary range: £15,000 to £30,000. If your airline posts you abroad, you'll get ex-pat living allowances.

Qualifications: GCSEs and A Levels often required; this isn't something you'd normally do as a first job; must be able to drive.

Will suit you if you: are sociable, good at talking and listening, lively, quick to absorb information, resourceful, well-organised and unflappable.

Perks: car, excellent discounts on any air travel for your holidays – typically 5 per cent or 10 per cent tickets.

Pitfalls: long hours; the bimbo factor affects both female and male executives: people sometimes assume that sales staff are dim-witted. 'The only way round it is to play up to it,' says one successful exec.

Future opportunities: move into general management or training in your airline; become an out-of-UK sales manager running your own station.

How to get in: • contact airlines direct for sales jobs or, failing those, in bookings or reservations departments (the classic route in) • see job ads and industry info in *Travel Trade Gazette* and *Travel Weekly*.

This is one of those jobs that makes other people wonder how you got to be so lucky: all the travel you could wish for, entertaining, company car . . .

But it is comparatively straightforward to become a sales executive on an international airline. Get any job with an airline and work your way up. Or gain sales experience from another area, and move across. 'There's a steep learning curve if you've come from outside the airline industry,' says one exec who did so.

This job does not usually involve hard selling. It's more of a PR role in which you inform travel agents and companies with a big travel budget about the services your airline provides, taking the travel agents and potential company clients on free trips to Barcelona, Barbados or wherever, to demonstrate the high standards of your airline.

As part of a team of execs, you'll be allocated a regional area of Britain. In your company car, you'll regularly visit and ring up to 400 travel agents, giving them updates on your airline: new routes, new deals, new incentives for the agents to promote your flights to clients. You'll read the *Financial Times* and trade magazines to find out which companies are setting up operations abroad, then try to pick up new lucrative clients whose staff you'll fly backwards and forwards.

Sales execs are each given a budget, to spend how they think best. You could find yourself taking clients abroad as much as three or four times a month. The next step is into your boss's shoes, managing the sales team, or moving into another part of the airline.

TEACHER OF ENGLISH AS A FOREIGN LANGUAGE

Working for: British Council, private and state language schools in UK and abroad.

Salary range: £5,500 to £40,000 (as a manager of a school).

Qualifications: you can get some teaching work without special training but there will be more job opportunities if you take one of a wide range of short courses (around four weeks full time). The most widely accepted are those leading to RSA/UCLES Certificate in TEFL (Teaching English as a Foreign Language) or the Trinity College Certificate, but there are others. Go for a school that's a member of ARELS (see below) and therefore accredited by the British Council. For those courses, you need to be over twenty with at least two A Levels, preferably a degree or a teacher's certificate.

Will suit you if you: are a good communicator and can get on with a wide range of people; have the ability to motivate, inspire and enthuse others; have a liking for English and an awareness of how we use it today.

Perks: the chance to work anywhere you choose in the world and learn new languages yourself; flexibility – choose your own hours.

Pitfalls: finding you've joined a 'cowboy outfit'; students getting out of hand.

Future opportunities: loads of jobs all over the world; you could become a manager of a school or even set up your own!

How to get in: • careers and courses info from The Association of Recognised English Language Services: send large SAE to ARELS, 2 Pontypool Place, Valentine Place, London SE1 8QF, tel 071–242 3136, 9.30 a.m.–5 p.m. • for posts in overseas schools and colleges: The British Council, OEAD, Medlock Street, Manchester M15 4PR • see job ads in *The Times Educational Supplement*, the *Guardian* on Tuesdays, and *EFL Gazette*.

English is arguably Britain's number one export, and has been for centuries. Millions of people worldwide want to speak our language, and believe that being taught by a Briton is the best way to learn.

You could be attached to a secondary school anywhere from Milan to Japan, or go into businesses to each executives in Paris and Madrid.

This is a job to be enjoyed for two or three years, but it also has the potential to become a long-term career tailored to your own particular interests. One teacher first spent two years in Tokyo through the British Council, then joined a private language school in Madrid, and now, at twenty-five, runs her own school in Barcelona. Others make use of other skills they've acquired – one teaches journalistic English to media students in Paris, while others, worldwide, teach English with a strong business slant.

TRANSLATOR

Working for: yourself, through translation agencies; some staff jobs with import/export companies, multinationals and the EC.

Salary range: £10,000 to £30,000; freelance rate approx. £50 per 1,000 words (overseas clients pay more).

Qualifications: a degree in your second language – universities of Salford, Bradford, Bath, UMIST and Herriot-Watt (Edinburgh) all run appropriate courses; ideally, practical experience of industry, and the country of your second tongue; the ability to write clear, contemporary English.

Will suit you if you: are self-motivated, interested in languages, happy to work on your own; can market your skills positively; get on with people.

Perks: you can travel if you want to; choose your own hours; no boss.

Pitfalls: the market is currently tough. Some of the technical stuff you'll be translating can get tediously repetitive and dull.

Future opportunities: it's an increasingly freelance market as companies cut down on overheads, but since trade between all countries is on the increase, so is the need to translate commercial documents.

How to get in: • send A4 SAE for careers and courses info to The Institute of Translation and Interpreting, 377 City Road, London EC1V 1NA, tel 071–713 7600, 9 a.m.–5 p.m. • contact translation agencies (names in *Yellow Pages*) • see job ads in the *Guardian* on Saturdays, and *ITA Bulletin* (in some libraries or from above address) • contact likely international organisations direct.

Forget about turning Proust and Anaïs Nin into eloquent English – most translating work required today is commercial. Companies who trade abroad want letters, legal documents, order forms, sales slips, invoices, and every other piece of business paper you can think of turned into the language their clients understand best – their own.

Since most companies can't afford a full-time foreign writer, they'll simply hire your services through an agency. It's ideal to start in one of these, and then go freelance. You may also specialise in technical, legal, medical or literary work.

Traditionally, translators are supposed only to translate into their mother tongue, from a second language. With dense documents, such as the instruction manual for a new German or Japanese computer, that is mainly still the case. But for shorter ones like letters and law-suit threats, you'll be turning English into Italian, German, French (fill in the language of your choice – all major ones have a market).

Be persistent with the agencies – once on their books follow up with phone calls. As a freelancer from home, you'll need the tools of your trade: a word processor, a fax machine, and stamina. You'll spend your days translating, quite quickly and very accurately, everything from legal documents to operating instructions for the latest kitchen gadget from abroad. Or you might get to do that blockbuster novel from Germany . . .

WINE BUYER

Working for: wine merchants/off-licences; supermarkets; department stores.

Salary range: £10,000 to £25,000 in wine merchants.

Qualifications: you can work your way up from sales assistant in a shop. A degree in an appropriate language/business is very useful; some employers want people who are educated to degree level (any subject), or who have A Levels.

Will suit you if you: enjoy wines and discovering new ones; have a commercial nose; are enthusiastic, a good negotiator and sociable.

Perks: free wine; travel to vineyards from Chile to Australia; introducing a new, wildly successful wine to Britain.

Pitfalls: you can drink too much in this business.

Future opportunities: rise in a supermarket; become an independent wine merchant; run your own wine bar; become a wine writer.

How to get in: • write to the personnel departments of off-licences and supermarket head offices • careers info from The Wine and Spirit Education Trust, Five Kings House, 1 Queen Street Place, London EC4R 1QS, tel 071–236 3351 • wine companies are listed in *The Wine & Spirit International Year Book*, in libraries • job ads in *Harper's Wine & Spirit Gazette*.

Apply for positions as a trainee wine buyer, and while you're waiting for an opening, take a job, any job, in an off-licence or wine wholesaler, is the advice of wine business employers. Read up about your subject in quality wine magazines and books. Don't miss any opportunities to learn more about wine. Companies like Oddbins help you to learn by holding regular tastings for their staff.

Many wine buyers start off on the sales floor of a shop and get into the wine-buying department at head office as soon as they are able, having developed a knowledge of different flavours by tasting, tasting, tasting. As a wine buyer, you'll travel from cellar to cellar for up to twenty weeks in the year, sampling wines, taking notes, going back to head office with recommendations or negotiating on the spot for suitable new additions to your company's stock. In a large company you're likely to specialise in a particular area – Australian wines, French clarets, or whatever. In smaller companies you could find your market is the world, encompassing South America, Europe, and Australia.

On the search for new wines, you'll be sent samples and go to trade tastings. You may even dream up a new wine that would fill a gap in the market, and get a supplier to realise it for you: a successful white wine, for example, could be developed into a sparkling one.

Back in the office, you'll spend your time making sure the wine supplies are delivered when they are supposed to be, and coming up with solutions if they're not. Periodically, you'll have to taste samples from your stock, to check the standard is still high.

All this will be done against a very commercial background: from the label to the wine itself, your choices must appeal and make a profit.

ZOOKEEPER

Working for: zoos, wildlife parks, safari parks, aquaria, dolphinaria.

Salary range: £130 per week for a seasonal trainee keeper (£190 in London) to £30,000 per annum for a curator (more managerial post).

Qualifications: some zoos require no formal ones; others, like London Zoo, specify that you must be eighteen or over with at least five good GCSEs including maths, English, and a science. If you want to rise in zoo management, it probably helps to have a degree: zoology or similar – plus, sometimes, a Masters or PhD. But everyone starts as a trainee keeper. In your early zoo years, you'll study for a City and Guilds Certificate in Zoo Animal Management. Safari park keepers need a driving licence.

Will suit you if you: have common sense; love and respect animals; can talk politely and informatively to visitors; have practical experience of animal care; don't mind hard work; can (later) manage others.

Perks: having contact with wild, rare animals; free entry to other zoos.

Pitfalls: being bitten by snakes etc.; dirty work (mucking out elephants) in cold conditions; pay is low at the start; unsocial hours; your zoo may be threatened with closure due to lack of funds.

Future opportunities: this is an exciting and changing field; there are interesting openings in wildlife parks, and conservation groups. You could collect endangered species for breeding; you could travel too.

How to get in: • contact The Institute of Zoology, Zoological Society of London, Regents Park, London NW1 4RY, tel 071–722 3333 for careers info, openings, list of zoos nationwide (A4 SAE preferred) • write directly to personnel departments of zoos you'd like to join • job vacancies in local papers, national papers, and specialist magazines such as *Aquarist and Pond Keeper, Cage and Aviary Bird.*

Office workers have to put up with reptiles and other beastly colleagues; in this job, the one breathing down your neck is likely to be a real crocodile or panther!

The best way in is to have clocked up some experience of working with animals – the actual species doesn't matter. Take Jill Hayward, at twenty-five a reptile keeper at Edinburgh Zoo. She did some 'barely paid' work with birds of prey and otters for private breeders before hand-delivering her application letter to Edinburgh Zoo. She left school at eighteen, with A Levels.

If you have a job like hers, it'll start at about 8.30 a.m., when you check up on all the animals in your section. You prepare the food – fresh greens for tortoises, insects for lizards, mice for snakes (but they only eat once or twice a fortnight). You feed, water and clean the cages and tanks, open up for the public, then spend most of the rest of the day in the backroom, tending newly hatched and sick animals, ordering fresh supplies of food and so on. In the summer, you collect greenfly for the lizards.

Jill's head keeper was recently offered a job in New Zealand: 'It's an international career,' she says. 'You can certainly travel.'

INFLUENCERS

If you're fascinated by the way the world is run, if you see faults and think you could do better given half a chance, this sector is for you. MPs and economists are people like the rest of us, with definite ideas about the smooth running of our country. You don't agree with their methods? The only way to beat them is to join them.

But influence can be a subtle thing: a word dropped in a journalist's ear, a report landing on a chairman's desk, can alter the course of business and of government. A timely conversation with an unhappy worker can alter the path of his or her career. These are the roles of campaigners, publicists, management consultants and careers counsellors.

What you need to change the world is a belief in your abilities, in the strength of your convictions, plus the knack of charming your opponents when it counts. In return you get the thrill of making a difference – because when you're in a position to influence, new laws may be passed, towns could be tidied up, rivers could be cleared, new foods could become the norm, companies could take on new enlightened policies . . .

You've got the power – enjoy it!

A&R MANAGER FOR A RECORD COMPANY

Working for: record companies such as EMI, Virgin, etc.

Salary range: talent scouts start on between £9,000 and £10,000. Managers on £20,000–£50,000+ depending on the success of the bands, so the sky's the limit.

Qualifications: none required. You just need experience in the music business in any shape or form – plus determination, and guile . . .

Will suit you if you: are obsessed with music; go out constantly to gigs; sociable; lively; have commercial and negotiating acumen.

Perks: being there; this is one of the most coveted positions in the music business. Huge income with all the trimmings, car etc., if you and your bands are a success.

Pitfalls: a cut-throat business: if you don't produce the goods you're out. Endless nights in smoky stuffy atmospheres not good for your health.

Future opportunities: if you tire of the corporate life, you could run your own record label, recording studio, or become an independent music agent.

How to get in: • get to know the record companies whose music you like and apply for any job within one; cultivate contacts where you can; there are, occasionally, student training programmes, so ask about those.

You've certainly got power and influence in this job. You, as artists and repertoire manager – always abbreviated to A&R – will be the one who listens to a band in a concert hall and decides if they're worth signing up (to be precise, talent scouts do most of the legwork). You will decide which record producer they should use, what style and image they should have, what songs they should sing. You, together with their road manager, will shape their careers. You'll also decide when to release them from their contracts if their records don't sell.

Ways into this business include: running a record shop and then, through knowing the sales reps of each record company, applying for any sales openings that come up – then working your way across to the A&R department. Or, like one of EMI's A&R managers, you could be in a successful band, then make the switch into the A&R department of the company that produces your records. Or get any job in the company and work upwards: secretary, production assistant . . .

'There's a lot of flexibility if you've got the right personality and know about music,' says one A&R co-ordinator (a non-creative, admin. role in the department). She did an HND in management studies then arranged 'opportune meetings' with A&R people at gigs.

Positions in the A&R departments are seriously coveted. People who have got in say they did it craftily, e.g. making friends with the A&R secretary, or co-ordinator, and finding out which bands the head of A&R will be at each evening . . . then turning up at the same gigs. It looks as though you're working hard and that you've got your finger on the pulse. And you do!

CAMPAIGNER

Working for: pressure groups such as Greenpeace, Amnesty International.

Salary range: £13,000 to £25,000.

Qualifications: no formal ones required; experience in a similar field, such as a month's unpaid work experience for a charity, and aptitude are considered more important. Must show campaigning and communication skills and knowledge of the campaign subject.

Will suit you if you: are enthusiastic and care for your subject; don't give up; can dream up good publicity schemes such as a sponsored celebrity walk or elephant ride across Britain to get your subject into the papers; can write and talk persuasively.

Perks: occasional travel in the UK and abroad; the kudos of seeing your campaign succeed; Greenpeace has environmentally friendly offices.

Pitfalls: dealing with toxic waste and some human slimeballs.

Future opportunities: there's room upwards in this increasingly professional sector; or you could move into commercial PR.

How to get in: • lots of job ads in the *Guardian* on Mondays and Saturdays • for general info send a large SAE to Amnesty International, 99 Rosebery Avenue, London EC1R 4RE and The Public Information Unit, Greenpeace Ltd, Canonbury Villas, London N1 2PN.

As a campaigner, you'll be raising money, awareness, changing laws and public opinion in the subject of your choice. The campaigner's prize is not cash. It's seeing injustices righted. Dolphins would still be widely caught in fishing nets if campaigners hadn't made a fuss and shamed tuna producers into becoming dolphin-friendly.

But getting your own way in the campaign world involves a lot of hard slogging. You could give a rousing speech to local fund-raisers one day and try to raise sponsorship at a meeting with a bigwig the next. In between you'll send avalanches of well-worded letters, talk to the press, liaise between various support groups and do the filing.

Michael Crowley, twenty-five, assistant to the head of campaigns at Amnesty International's UK office, got his job by turning up at the offices for voluntary work. 'I just knocked on the door and asked for Personnel.' Before you pack your lunch box, Amnesty says this is no longer a way in. 'But even if you can't get a job in the organisation of your choice, clocking up that voluntary experience will help you get a post elsewhere,' reckons Michael. Other campaigners agree.

Personnel officers say the key to getting a campaigner's job is to show an understanding of the subject, whether it's unfair imprisonment, whale hunting, water pollution, thinning of the ozone layer, importation of threatened exotic birds . . . there are certainly enough areas to choose from. The fastest way to get informed is to read the quality papers, and send off for campaign information from the organisation you would like to join.

Then start your first campaign: to get yourself a job.

CAREERS COUNSELLOR

Working for: careers consultancy companies; yourself as a freelance consultant.

Salary range: £20,000 to £30,000 is common but up to £80,000.

Qualifications: none required (some big companies ask for a degree, subject not important). In practice, each counsellor has their own unique blend of work experience and qualifications which they bring to the job.

Will suit you if you: are caring, analytical, empathetic, mature; have a positive attitude; can listen patiently and come up with practical steps for people who may be low on hope or self-esteem; have yourself learnt from a range of experience; are in your mid-twenties or older and willing to learn new skills.

Perks: seeing people's lives transformed after counselling.

Pitfalls: redundancy counselling can get you down, but you must stay positive.

Future opportunities: redundancy and general counselling is mushrooming.

How to get in: • contact careers counselling companies direct: one large company is KPMG Career Consultancy Services, PO Box 730, 20 Farringdon Street, London EC4A 4PP • send A4 SAE to The Institute of Careers Guidance, 27a Lower High Street, Stourbridge, West Midlands DY8 1TA, tel (0384) 376464.

Careers counsellors are not to be confused with careers officers. Officers are employed by local education authorities to talk to school- and college-leavers and other individuals about their career options. Officers train at one of fifteen centres around the UK, and need some kind of college education first. If you want to join them, ask your local careers officer, listed in the phone book under your local authority, or contact the Institute (see above).

Counsellors, in contrast, come from a whole range of different backgrounds. It's a much newer occupation which sprang up to answer the demands of job-hunting today. Most counsellors have gained experience in several areas of work before joining a consultancy. Some study psychology first – and that gives a clue to the character of the job: as a counsellor, you are trying to get your clients to understand why they're not happy in their present careers, and help them to find the right career for them, or to improve their current one.

Tick-the-box psychometric tests come into it, but mainly as a back-up to a counsellor's own assessment of someone's character. A typical counsellor (if one exists) would spend some of their time taking seminars on company premises, and some of it talking one-to-one with clients. On the increase for obvious reasons is what's known as 'outplacement counselling' – helping people cope with redundancy and find a new direction. KPMG is prominent in this field.

Broadly speaking, on the basis that you need to have lived a bit to understand others' dilemmas, counselling consultancies prefer you to have had some experience of the world first.

CHARTERED SECRETARY

Working for: big businesses; local government; other large institutions.

Salary range: part-qualified – £12,000 to £16,000; qualified – £19,000 to £35,000+.

Qualifications: if you're seventeen or over you can start the ICSA (Institute of Chartered Secretaries and Administrators) course at foundation level, with no previous academic qualifications. Graduates or people with relevant work experience go in at a higher level. The course involves up to five years' study part-time and covers law, finance, information system management, committee administration – the skills you need to organise big businesses.

Will suit you if you: enjoy administrating and organising; are diplomatic, with excellent people skills, a problem-solver, good with figures, patient.

Perks: company car, health scheme.

Pitfalls: people misunderstanding your role: 'I am not a secretary!' you will be tempted to yell at them.

Future opportunities: Perhaps because this is a relatively low profile career, there are good opportunities to rise within it. Reach a top position in a multi-national company; or use your knowledge of business practices to set up your own company; or become a management consultant.

How to get in: • contact The Institute of Chartered Secretaries and Administrators, 16 Park Crescent, London W1N 4AH, tel 071–580 4741, 9.30 a.m.–5.30 p.m. • see job ads in *The Administrator*.

This career doesn't have an awful lot to do with being a secretary, though many who flourish in this career did start out with secretarial skills.

As a very rough guide, you'll be a sort of manager, administrator and secretary rolled into one effective, and high-powered position. You may be responsible for the overall management of several departments within your company. You may do the planning and paperwork necessary to start a new office overseas. You may bring in a new computer system, working with a systems analyst to ensure that the present and future needs of your organisation will be satisfied by the new package. You could oversee the accounts department, or act as a general troubleshooter when a particular department, such as sales, or personnel, goes off the rails. And to help you do any or all of these things, your training will have given you experience of how these departments all function.

You can go as high as chairman in this job . . . or go travelling if you prefer. One recent job ad was for a corporate services supervisor for an international bank in Bermuda: the post involved supervisory skills, strong technical ability, and developed communication skills. Not to mention a liking for sun tans!

CONFERENCE ORGANISER

Working for: conference firms; a large general business; yourself.

Salary range: £11,000 to £30,000.

Qualifications: education to A Level standard usually required; typing skills.

Will suit you if you: are highly organised and get things done, patient, willing to muck in when the rush is on, sociable, upbeat, smart, charming, full of ideas, aware of current events; have a commercial nose.

Perks: the rush of adrenalin is similar to that experienced when organising a major party; fulfilling to see what was just an idea turn into a room full of 700 delegates.

Pitfalls: a speaker who fails to turn up; delegates who moan; some unsocial hours.

Future opportunities: a long-term growth area: businesses see conferences as a relatively cheap way of assimilating the latest information and management methods.

How to get in: • contact conference organisers direct – look in the phone book • read trade magazines and see who organised the conferences they write about • contact recruitment agents, many of whom specialise (one that does is Albany Appointments, 5 Dering Street, London W1R 9AB).

Dotted around Britain, right now, are 500 to 1,000 business people who are longing to learn new ways to motivate their staff. They may not even *know* they want to learn these yet, but they will. Because you, conference organiser extraordinaire, are going to persuade them.

Conference organisers operate in different ways according to the size of their team, the kind of conferences in which they specialise, and so on. But this will be your basic work:

You will read the trade press, watch the news, keep your eyes out generally for the new buzz words and fashionable new management concepts that circulate regularly around the business community. Then, when you've located a subject area you think may be of interest in a year's time (you work far ahead, because it takes time to organise and publicise), you will call on a few business people, and try out the idea on them. Depending on their reactions, you will adapt your plans and put them into motion.

You will have to book a suitable venue and speakers, and organise the printing of a publicity brochure with application form which will be mailed to likely people, and inserted into their regular trade magazines. You'll hire the services of sound technicians, and caterers to sweeten your delegates' humour with a tasty lunch and wine. You'll gather your speakers together for a meeting one month before the day, to check that Mr X is not planning to say the same thing as Ms Y. Then you're ready for the fun to begin.

On the day you'll make sure it all runs smoothly. But, afterwards, you don't relax: you have up to 20 other projects to organise that same year.

ECONOMIST

Working for: Civil Service (including EC posts), big businesses, financial institutions, local government.

Salary range: Civil Service pay from £5,500 (Cadets) or £13,000 (economic assistant) up to £48,000. In the private sector, the sky's the limit.

Qualifications: a good economics degree or similar from one of a wide range of universities and colleges, including, of course, the London School of Economics.

Will suit you if you: are numerate, analytical; can turn columns of figures into a forecast of what is likely to happen to businesses, society, the economy over the next few years; can turn jargon into plain English.

Perks: good pension in the Civil Service; car and other corporate trimmings in private sector.

Pitfalls: you're the Cassandra of the twentieth century: you can foresee doom and recessions etc., but no one seems to take a blind bit of notice; and economic forecasts involve such complex, ever-changing equations, you can get your predictions wrong anyway.

Future opportunities: fairly limited openings for pure economists. You can move profitably into general management, financial market research.

How to get in: • shop around the universities for suitable degree courses; check out the London School of Economics and Political Science, Houghton Street, London WC2A 2AE, tel 071–405 7686 • for a career in the Civil Service/EC, contact Recruitment & Assessment Services, Alencon Link, Basingstoke, Hants RG21 1JB, tel (0256) 846306 • read *The Economist* for industry info and job ads.

Here's something you never predicted when you were still doing your A Levels: that one day you'd be sitting bold as brass in the House of Commons, telling ministers a thing or two about the economy . . .

As an economist with the Civil Service, it goes with the job. Your role is to give information on demand about current job trends, import/export ratios and anything else ministers may need to know to formulate new policies. You might prepare and analyse new taxation options for the next budget, or advise on how much or how little investment should be put into Britain's highways. And you have to provide the information within hours.

The Civil Service is the largest single employer of economists, but there are openings in big business too. In a financial institution, you could become an investment or credit analyst, digging into a company's financial affairs to decide, basically, whether or not your bank should lend them money.

It's not just a question of looking at company accounts, though that comes into it. You'll be tuned into industry gossip. As one senior City analyst says, 'You have to do the research but in the end it comes down to a hunch.' So you have to be an excellent judge of people and resist the temptation to follow the crowd. The wisest economists in recent years were the ones who took the decision *not* to lend to Robert Maxwell.

ENVIRONMENTAL HEALTH OFFICER/ ADVISER

Working for: district councils; large companies and environmental organisations; yourself as a freelance consultant.

Salary range: £15,000 to £20,000; directors up to £50–60,000.

Qualifications: diploma in environmental health (three-year course with work experience in district council environment office) or degree in environmental health/environmental sciences (see addresses below).

Will suit you if you: care about the environment; are analytical, numerate, a problem-solver, diplomatic.

Perks: improving the environment and people's well-being.

Pitfalls: can be distressing visiting badly run abattoirs, or slums; in companies your employers may ignore recommendations.

Future opportunities: thousands of posts in district councils; commercial and industrial companies are hiring environmental health officers and environmental advisers; or you could move to a pressure group.

How to get in: • careers and courses info from The Institution of Environmental Health Officers, 16 Great Guildford St, London SE1 0ES, tel 071–928 6006, 9 a.m.–1 p.m., 2–6 p.m. (A4 SAE preferred) • courses info from The Institution of Environmental Sciences, 14 Princes Gate, Hyde Park, London SW7 1PU, tel 081–766 6755 • contact green charities and pressure groups of your choice.

Environmental health officers monitor the bad elements of our environment, and come up with solutions to bring them to acceptable standards. It's not for the squeamish, because by necessity you have to visit the muckiest, dankest, dirtiest parts of Britain in order to improve them.

Note: environmental health officers and environmental advisers are not the same thing – though you could end up doing the same job. To work for local government, you train as an environmental health officer; to work elsewhere, you choose from a range of courses, or do an environmental health course.

First steps for the latter: try to get accepted as a student EHO by a district council, who will then pay you a salary during your training, and, of course, offer you work experience. Otherwise simply do the course and get a post afterwards.

You're an environmental detective and troubleshooter. You can choose to be a generalist, a sort of gunge-buster, or you can concentrate on a particular area: waste disposal, or noise pollution, or old dilapidated housing. In a company, you might advise on environmentally sound improvements to the workplace; in a pressure group, you might measure waste being discharged into the sea.

This is an area that gets the glare of publicity . . . but long after the TV cameras have gone, you'll be there, implementing solutions.

FASHION BUYER

Working for: large boutiques and department stores.

Salary range: sales assistants £8,000 to £9,000; trainee buyers £11,000; buyers £18,000 to £45,000+.

Qualifications: none required except an ability to do the job. It's the norm to move up from the sales floor (though it's a hard climb). There are a few graduate trainee schemes but you'd have to be 'bloody marvellous', to quote one industry observer, to get in that way.

Will suit you if you: have an eye for fashion, spotting trends before they've formed; are a good negotiator and analyst, a tireless shopper; can keep a secret (or your rivals will rip off your ideas); have a commercial nose.

Perks: 20 per cent discounted clothes; profit-share schemes; travel; car.

Pitfalls: job cuts in bad times.

Future opportunities: if you clear the first hurdle of actually getting in, you could eventually rise to managerial level or to the board of a large chain; move into market research or fashion journalism; run your own business; become a BUYER for an environmentally green retailer.

How to get in: • apply to all shops whose styles appeal to you – be prepared to start in sales, and work your way up • there are some suitable courses – check out the BTEC HND in Business of Fashion Management at The London College of Fashion, 20 John Prince's Street, London W1M 0BJ, tel 071–629 9401 • pick up the best fashion work experience wherever you can.

To get into this business today you need the tenacity of a fashion addict clawing their way into an overcrowded Paris fashion show. Which is just as well because that's precisely what you will sometimes be required to do.

As a fashion buyer, you'll spend a lot of time travelling: you could be a regular at the haute couture shows in London, Paris, Milan, America and Japan. You visit a huge number of fashion manufacturers in the UK and abroad. Your aim, quite simply, is to shop. You're shopping on behalf of your customers, guessing what they're going to want to wear a season or two ahead. And – it's every shopper's dream – you could be spending millions.

You'll analyse the buying patterns of your customers, build on classic lines that sell and sell, and bring in transient fashions. You'll have to decide what's required, track it down (you will travel to some wholesalers, others will court you); negotiate the best deals from desirable sources. There will even be an element of design coming from you, as you develop new fashion ideas in conjunction with your suppliers.

The fashion press, such as *Drapers Record*, is required reading, to help you tune into rising trends. Your biggest nightmare will be the risks that didn't pay: a conviction that spots will sell can turn into an embarrassing pile of sale clothing. Too many of those mistakes, and you'll be out too. Especially in times of recession, your career can hang on a thread.

FOOD BUYER

Working for: shops, supermarkets, food halls of department stores.

Salary range: £12,000 to £17,000 to start; up to £40,000 for a manager; up to a maximum of £70,000 for a departmental director.

Qualifications: entry on three levels: working your way up from the most junior position in the company; after A Levels or after a degree (subject not important) as an assistant/trainee buyer. The most qualified move up fastest.

Will suit you if you: are interested in food; like eating out a lot; collect new ways of cooking things; are imaginative; a good communicator, tuned into food fashions, curious, organised, have a commercial sense.

Perks: sampling a whole range of foods and drinks; discounted shopping; some travel; seeing one of your meal ideas become a success.

Pitfalls: having to taste ten curries the morning after a wild night!

Future opportunities: the chilled/convenience food market is growing; people always want new, easy-to-prepare foods and buyers have good promotion prospects. You could set up your own food supply business; run a restaurant.

How to get in: • contact personnel at head offices of major supermarket companies.

By 9.30 a.m., you, as food buyer, will have checked by computer that all the foods that were due in by last night have arrived. If a lorry's broken down or supplies haven't arrived for any other reason, you'll also have sorted out a solution, perhaps ordering double for tomorrow.

Then it's into a busy schedule of tastings, phone calls and meetings, meetings, meetings. There'll probably be two tastings in the morning, where you and one or two of your colleagues go to the home economist's kitchen and sample dishes they've cooked up. Some of these will be routine checks on products the store is already selling. Others will be new ideas, still in the development stage. (You never taste alone, because a consensus of opinion is what you're after.)

New ideas are an important part of the food buyer's work load. Half of these will come from suppliers, who may have found a particular dish of theirs is doing very well in restaurants, for example. The other half will be dreamed up by you and your team.

Cindy Baker, thirty-two, is deputy buying manager for ready meals, pasta, desserts and coffee shop at Sainsbury's. She did A Levels, then joined as a general management trainee before switching to food buying. 'It's very much a team process; we have brainstorming meetings,' she says. 'For example, we saw foods with tikka flavour were doing well, so came up with tikka bread.'

You'll liaise with the food scientists and packaging departments as your products develop. You'll also visit factories to ensure the best products for your company. Suppliers are understandably keen to have large orders from supermarkets, and will court you as a result. 'One of the first things you learn is how to handle the power,' says Cindy.

IMAGE CONSULTANT

Working for: yourself, giving advice to business people, private clients.

Salary range: from £8,000 to £30,000+. Typical consultation fee: £50 for 1½–2 hours.

Qualifications: none required in this fairly new area – but you'll need something on which to build a reputation. It's usual to do a private course: CMB Image Consultants (Color Me Beautiful) does a twelve-day one costing £2,500. It sends you off with the business equipment you need – drapes, colour wheels etc. You'll also need a suitable, light room at home for your studio.

Will suit you if you: have a strong visual sense, an eye for colour, a sense of fashion and of realism (you can't force someone to go against their basic character); are sympathetic, empathetic and have good communication skills; are able to instil confidence in others; are self-disciplined, motivated, commercially minded, and mature (this is an ideal second career).

Perks: be your own boss; work your own hours; transform people.

Pitfalls: onus is on you to build up the business; you can feel isolated; pricy to start.

How to get in: • shop around for suitable private courses. They cost you, but you may get a grant, or a Career Development Loan (telephone twenty-four-hour freephone 0800 585505). Word of mouth is a good recommendation for courses, though what suits someone else may not suit you. Try CMB Image Consultants, 66 Abbey Business Centre, Ingate Place, London SW8 3NS, tel 071–627 5211 • contact established image consultants with excellent reputations; ask to be their assistant/do work experience.

If you ever need to read the news on television, do this before you start: lift your shoulders up, wriggle about a bit in your chair, then straighten up and get ready for the cameras to roll.

That's just one of the tricks an image consultant might pass on to a newscaster, or indeed anyone else who has to appear on TV. The little movement enables you to feel more comfortable and look more natural too.

Image consultants are products of our televisual age, but it's only in the last decade that they've really come into their own. A common way to start is through a course with an umbrella organisation – CMB with 200 consultants throughout the UK is one of the biggest. Not quite a franchise, you buy supplies from CMB but operate independently.

In one-to-one consultations, you'll give advice on colour, shape, cloth, cut, accessories, body language, and you'll give clients a colour card to help them go for the most flattering shades. You may even take them shopping.

Image consultant Julia Scowsill has found the best way to build up new business is to offer seminars to companies and other groups. Appointments for individual consultations invariably follow.

MANAGEMENT CONSULTANT

Working for: a consultancy or yourself, advising companies on how to improve their management methods.

Salary range: some graduates start on £13,000; otherwise, £16,000 to £40,000; can go up to £150,000, even £300,000.

Qualifications: good A Levels and a good degree is the norm, though you could also get in with sound managerial experience but no academic qualifications. In practice, most people do this as a second career; there are also openings in large consultancies (e.g. KPMG Peat Marwick) for graduates straight from college.

Will suit you if you: can observe, absorb and analyse the ways in which individual businesses operate, and come up with realistic improvements; have an enquiring mind; are diplomatic; have excellent people skills; are methodical, numerate, empathetic, mature, and an astute negotiator.

Perks: good pay package; company car.

Pitfalls: employees in the workplaces you visit are often suspicious and unhelpful so it's up to you to win them over; long hours; tons of paperwork.

Future opportunities: established management consultants tend to specialise in one area – information technology, management buyouts – and never need be out of work.

How to get in: • good careers info from The Institute of Management Consultants, 32 Hatton Garden, London EC1N 8DL, tel 071–242 2140, 8.30 a.m.–5.30 p.m. • contact individual management consultancies.

'The industry has got slimmer recently: I estimate there are approximately 15 per cent fewer people employed in management consultancy than there were two years ago,' is the opinion of one recruitment consultant.

It's not hard to see why: management consultancy was a hip thing in the 1980s. Back then, businesses were expanding and liked nothing better than to invite consultants in to analyse their working methods and recommend how they could be improved. By 1990, when businesses were getting strapped for cash . . . when they needed help most, they could least afford it.

That said, management consultancy is a long-term growth industry, with openings for young, bright specialists with a background in accountancy, business practices, marketing and sales, personnel or other areas of commerce and industry.

If you join a firm of management consultants, you are likely to receive several months of training on the job, working under the guidance of a senior colleague. Here are some examples of the work you'd do as a fully fledged consultant: a greeting card company calls you in to advise on a new system of incentives to increase productivity; a transport company has a disturbingly high staff turnover – you go in as a troubleshooter, work out what's going wrong, and stop the rot; another company is short of managers – you go in for a month to work as a managerial temp.

MEMBER OF PARLIAMENT

Working for: Government; representing your constituency's interests in the House of Commons.

Salary range: All MPs are on £30,854; Cabinet Ministers earn more; Prime Minister earns £76,234. And all receive living, travel and office allowances.

Qualifications: you have to become a member of a political party, then be accepted as a candidate by a constituency, then be voted into Parliament.

Will suit you if you: have a wide general knowledge; care about the way the country and your constituency are run; are a persuasive debater, quick-witted, tough, and an effective campaigner; inspire confidence in others; are charismatic, indomitable, and a tireless networker.

Perks: MPs often have 'interests', i.e. salaries, from various companies for various functions – usually advisory. You and your family get a certain amount of free travel between home/constituency and London.

Pitfalls: your party could be toppled from power at any moment; you throw yourself into running as a candidate and then don't get elected . . . you have to start over again; relationships can suffer; insults from everyone.

Future opportunities: ex-MPs have plenty of juicy offers to go into industry. You could become big as a campaigner; hit the lecture circuit.

How to get in: • contact your local constituency party • contact head offices: The Labour Party, 150 Walworth Road, London SE17 1JT; Conservative Central Office, 32 Smith Square, London SW1P 3HH; Liberal Democrats, 4 Cowley Street, London SW1P 3NB. • send for general info from The Public Information Service, House of Commons, London SW1A 0AA, tel 071–219 4272 • get a job as a researcher for an MP – see ads in national press, or through the parties.

'PRIVATE AND CONFIDENTIAL: APPLICATION FOR CONSIDERATION AS AN APPROVED CONSERVATIVE CANDIDATE' says the white form from the Conservative Central Office.

Being an MP is not a rarefied business: anyone can send off and apply to the party of their choice. The Tory Party emphasises the fact that you need three good referees, including an MP, a constituency chairman, and perhaps someone suitably high-powered like the chairman of a multinational firm in your area. The Labour Party offers helpful advice: 'Most MPs will have acquired the necessary experience from working as councillors, or from working in their trade unions, tenants' association or other groups.'

Once you've been active for a while in your local party (Labour say two years' membership is required); you can then apply to become a candidate. Each party effectively has a shopping list from which local constituencies choose their candidates. Come election time, you may become one of the 650 people elected. You'll spend one day a week in the constituency, dealing with voters' queries and problems, and much of the rest of the time in the House, debating new laws. You'll also be courted by people who want you to use your influence on their behalf (see also PR/PARLIAMENTARY LOBBYIST).

PR OFFICER/ PARLIAMENTARY LOBBYIST

Working for: public relations firms; large companies and organisations; yourself.

Salary range: assistant account executive in a consultancy – £10,000 to £12,000. Then usually up to £30,000 or £40,000; for some, the sky's the limit.

Qualifications: 50 per cent of the Institute of Public Relations' members are graduates. Academic qualifications *can* help you get into jobs, but the main requirement is the ability to *do* the job. (Typing skills and being able to stuff endless press releases quickly into envelopes both useful . . .)

Will suit you if you: have excellent people skills; know your subject; can turn jargon into plain English; are persuasive, enthusiastic, determined, an accomplished networker; can absorb and act on information quickly.

Perks: depends on the job – if you're publicising a travel firm to journalists, you'll have free trips to exotic locations; a cosmetics PR worker would have endless samples of the latest make-up products; entertaining; a car.

Pitfalls: job cuts in bad times; the bimbo factors – some misguided people will treat you as though you're on the dim side.

Future opportunities: more openings here than in its neighbouring field, journalism. Once you've acquired the skills and experience, and if you've got the right temperament, you could start your own consultancy.

How to get in: • send A5 SAE for good careers info to The Institute of Public Relations, The Old Trading House, 15 Northburgh Street, London EC1V 0PR; tel 071–253 5151, 9.30 a.m.–5.30 p.m. • consult *Hollis* (in libraries) for addresses of consultancies • see job ads in the *Guardian* on Mondays, and *PR Week*.

There's a wonderful firm in the Midlands, which makes a new fabric that flatters every figure . . . but no one knows about it, so no one buys it. Enter: the PR – the public relations practitioner.

As a PR, your role in the hypothetical company above is to publicise their innovative new product. You send journalists press releases which tell them about the new product, ring them up and offer them free trips to the factory. Articles may then appear in the trade magazines. Other articles are published in women's magazines and newspapers. The success of your campaign will be measured in column inches of editorial coverage.

PRs don't just promote products, though. You might be working in a similar way to change the image of a company, or lobbying MPs and other influential figures so your clients' interests are catered for in new laws being debated in Parliament. This is the discreetly powerful realm of the parliamentary lobbyist, adept at networking in high places.

PERSONNEL MANAGER

Working for: any large organisation that employs people – manufacturing companies, hotels, department stores, airlines, health services, local authorities . . .

Salary range: from £9,000 to £70,000, but mostly between £17,000 and £30,000.

Qualifications: none required at start. Move from a secretarial post to one in personnel, or enter direct from university. The Institute of Personnel Management (IPM) offers on-the-job courses which help promotion prospects.

Will suit you if you: enjoy bringing out the best in people, and can empathise with them; are good at listening; are analytical and problem-solving.

Perks: large companies offer bonuses, health schemes, training, travel discounts (and it'll be your job to suggest and implement all perks!)

Pitfalls: you could be pig-in-the-middle between management and staff.

Future opportunities: wide and varied – you'll be able to move between very different companies, from airlines to zoos. Or you could run your own training company or recruitment agency, or be a personnel consultant.

How to get in: • send a large SAE for careers and courses info to The Institute of Personnel Management, IPM House, Camp Road, London SW19 4UX • write on spec to the personnel departments of large organisations you'd like to join • see job ads in *Personnel Management* and *PM Plus*.

A catering assistant has just walked into your office in tears because the financial director has threatened her with the sack for not serving meals promptly in the directors' dining room. Your job is to: a) calm the assistant b) calm the director c) let it be known diplomatically to both parties that this company is run professionally and firing is only done along certain, agreed lines d) with the catering manager, come up with a solution to late meals.

As personnel officer, your daily challenge is to try to ensure that your organisation is run in an orderly fashion that maximises the well-being of the staff and hence the success of the company.

Personnel managers don't just sort out spats between workers and management. You interview candidates for jobs, liaising with managers to find out their requirements, and sending the best candidates on to them for final interviews. You could also get involved with making your company's office environmentally friendly, with air-conditioning, comfortable chairs and decent working hours. 'I helped to design a new "green" office building, and it was the most rewarding part of my work,' says one twenty-nine-year-old personnel manager at a multinational computer company.

TOWN AND COUNTRY PLANNER

Working for: town planning departments of local authorities.

Salary range: trainees £9,000; qualified £10,000 to £25,000.

Qualifications: most first get a degree in town planning (or any degree, then do a conversion course); or start as a school-leaver and train by day release while on the job.

Will suit you if you: have a good feel for 'people' politics; care for the environment; have a natural 'presence' or can cultivate one; are realistic; can negotiate and be diplomatic.

Perks: Car, relocation, travel expenses depending on the local authority.

Pitfalls: things can get sticky when you're in a meeting with 500 angry villagers protesting against a proposed new airport. Some developers try to put the pressure on as well.

Future opportunities: usually jobs to be had – two months after graduating, 80 per cent of the students on one course at the University of Strathclyde had planning jobs. Contact lots of local authorities, or use your skills in campaigning and PR.

How to get in: • careers and courses info from the Secretary General, Royal Town Planning Institute, 26 Portland Place, London W1N 4BE (A5 SAE optional), tel 071–636 9107, 9 a.m.–4.30 p.m.

As a town planner working for a town or county council you'll be influencing where the people in your region live, work, shop and play . . . right down to where they park their cars.

Land is a limited resource and a whole range of people – property developers, road builders, hypermarket owners – want to turn green fields into concrete. The town planner must strike a balance between protecting the countryside and giving the go-ahead to useful projects. You talk to interested parties, study reports about the area, visit sites, then turn down or approve an application as you see fit.

But town planners have to be realistic, or their decisions may be overridden by vested interests, by government. You must persuade developers and conservationists to agree on one plan to the benefit of all.

Joan McGarvey, who graduated a year ago from the University of Strathclyde, explains: 'You need to be politically aware for this job – that should be an element of any course you apply to do.'

You may hold meetings with the waste disposal department to check that waste is being buried where it's supposed to be. Or you may discuss plans with local councillors, developers, conservationists, for a new conservation area. 'There's a lot of talking,' explains Joan. 'And you're dealing with senior people from your first day in this job. So you have to carve a position for yourself, to make sure they take notice of you.'

MONEY, MONEY, MONEY

Make it, spend it, save it, invest it . . . you know what to do with money. And that means every working person in this land, from pop stars to police departments, from flower shops to film companies, needs help and advice from you.

Whether it's as an accountant, bank manager, agent or shop manager, when you're in the money business you're helping to keep the economy moving – or even helping to kick start it, in today's slow climate. And the perks are often pure gold.

But it's more than mere pounds and pennies. If you like playing mental games; are good at understanding the human factor behind the financial figures; if you don't get fazed handling sums far bigger than your annual salary . . . this could be the sector for you.

ACCOUNTANT/ FINANCIAL MANAGER

Working for: accountancy firms; all types of businesses; NHS and local government.

Salary range: £9,000 (while training) to £80,000+.

Qualifications: two A Levels, with maths and English among your GCSEs, or a similar qualification. Many have a degree; the subject doesn't matter. You'll join either a firm of accountants, or any type of large company, or a local government department. Once there, you can study for the necessary accountancy exams, by block release, or by correspondence for three years, or four if you need to do a foundation course first. (See addresses below.)

Will suit you if you: understand numbers and business; are meticulous; will stick to a task till it's done; are good at communicating.

Perks: get paid a decent salary while you train!

Pitfalls: people often think it's a dull career – but it needn't be.

Future opportunities: excellent. Run your own business or rise to the top of a large one; become a partner in an accountancy firm.

How to get in: • contact The Institute of Chartered Accountants, Moorgate Place, London EC2P 2BJ, tel 071–628 7060 9.15–5.15 p.m. for info including courses • contact The Institute of Chartered Accountants of Scotland, 27 Queen Street, Edinburgh EH2 1LA, tel 031–225 5673, 9–5 p.m. • Chartered Association of Certified Accountants, 29 Lincoln's Inn Fields, London WC2A 3EE, tel 071–242 6855 9–5.30 p.m. • Chartered Institute of Public Finance and Accountancy, 3 Robert Street, London WC2N 6BH, tel 071–895 8823 9–5 p.m. for good info on careers in the NHS and local authorities. You can get more details from careers officers.

Accountants may have a restrained appearance but career options are limitless.

Basically, anywhere there are people and funds, there's possible work for you. So after qualifying you could join the staff of a theatre, TV, film company – or apply to train with any big retail chain. You'll help to run the accounts of your company on a day-to-day basis – devising budgets, keeping financial records, making sure tax, VAT and National Insurance contributions are up to date.

Or, like many, you might choose to train with a firm of accountants such as Touche Ross or Arthur Andersen (see the phone book – use the London one in your local library if such firms aren't listed in your area). With them, you could spend much of your time going into a range of companies to audit, or check, their yearly accounts to see the income and outgoings balance, and that tax, including VAT payments, are in order.

One flourishing area is financial management for the NHS: working for a local health authority anywhere from Devon to Aberdeen, you'll devise budgets with doctors and nurses, and oversee big spending plans for new hospital developments.

ADVERTISING ACCOUNT EXECUTIVE

Working for: advertising agencies.

Salary range: from £12,000 up to £150,000 (account director).

Qualifications: a good degree (this shouldn't strictly be necessary but the competition is such that agencies invariably go for graduates; non-grads can always try to change their minds though). Degree subject not important; agencies like a mix among their staff).

Will suit you if you: are bright and self-motivated; can manage people; are assertive, responsible, a teamworker; have a strong commercial sense; appreciate the creative process; are persuasive; can handle pressure.

Perks: a flash car; entertaining; larger agencies give free membership of health club and bonuses.

Pitfalls: stress of juggling demanding clients; too much corporate entertaining is bad for the health; serious competition from colleagues.

Future opportunities: people tend to spend their whole career in their agencies – or start their own. Jump over the fence into a marketing position with one of your client companies, or move into publishing.

How to get in: • write to advertising agencies direct • read *Campaign* for industry info and job ads • info from CAM Foundation, Abford House, 15 Wilton Road, London SW1V 1NJ, tel 071–828 7506, 9.30 a.m.–5.30 p.m.

If you've heard how hard it is to enter advertising, take heart from this: 'There's a big battle for the best candidates every year,' says the recruitment director of one major agency. 'We have often found that other agencies have also made offers to the really good ones.'

That said, the smaller agencies in particular have cut back on their recruitment. This is what you'll need to succeed: get a good degree; apply to all the agencies that appeal to you; come across as keen, motivated, bright, full of ideas, a good manager of people . . . and someone who understands and fits in with that agency's own particular style. That means you should have been reading the industry publications, studying ads, and talking to people in advertising whenever you can.

As account executive, or account manager, you're the linchpin of the whole advertising process. You're the one who maintains day-to-day contact between the client, and the creative and production teams in your agency. You're 'co-ordinating the various team players so that the process of advertising development happens effectively', as the recruitment information from Ogilvy & Mather has it.

You'll be responsible for a handful of accounts. Just one of the daily challenges might be taking a phone call from a client who is worried about an ad which is on the verge of being released, and which the client's directors have decided they don't like. You'll come up with a solution. And when you're not doing things like that, you're pitching for new accounts.

AGENT

Working for: yourself. Your clients will be from one of these groups: actors, authors, models, musicians/singers, make-up artists, record producers, voice-overs, etc.

Salary range: a percentage of your clients' earnings: from 10–40 per cent. Junior model bookers start at around £7,000; assistants to other agents £10,000 to £12,000. Agents make from £20,000 to £200,000, depending on their client list.

Qualifications: none whatsoever, apart from extensive inside knowledge of your business. People in the more literary areas – books, plays, films – would usually have a degree. All assistants need secretarial skills.

Will suit you if you: are an astute judge of talent before it's fully developed, a good negotiator, self-motivated; care about your subject and keep learning more; are sociable, pleasant . . . but tough.

Perks: be your own boss, work your own hours; entertaining and travel.

Pitfalls: nurturing bright talents, then having them poached by other agents when they become famous; late payments; getting it wrong.

Future opportunities: depend entirely on you, and your clients.

How to get in: • ask agents in your subject area for assistants' jobs (if you're not sure how to locate agents, ask in your library: it will stock a number of trade directories which give names and addresses of agents in specific fields, such as acting, art, music, writing etc) • clock up experience in a creative industry then, when you've got the knowledge, set up on your own.

Agents have been accused of being rather parasitic, living off the talents of their naive but gifted, creative clients. But the reality is that agents and artists make successful partners, both rising further in their careers than they would if they operated independently.

As an agent, it's your job to be the commercially canny one in the relationship. If you're a literary agent, it means cultivating good new publishing contacts, introducing your clients to suitable publishers, negotiating contracts, generally looking after your authors' interests (because their interests are your own). If you're a model agent, it means finding work and settling fees, making sure the models aren't ripped off and they don't take up jobs that would be inappropriate to their career. In all agency work, you help your clients to become more professional, more marketable, and you get them the best deals possible.

To do all this you need good inside knowledge of your industry – which is why many first work within it, then switch to being an agent. You need credibility, so draw on the appropriate expertise to make yourself look authoritative: get your basic contract drawn up by an expert; have your business letterhead designed to look right.

You need to keep abreast of information and gossip, so you know what the going rates are. But if you don't know something, ask, and people will tell you. You have to be tough to deal with pressures from would-be artists, a few grasping publishers, journalists who would interview your famous clients every hour of the day if they could . . . and after all that you still have to do the VAT returns and balance the books.

BANK MANAGER

Working for: the major clearing banks: Barclays, Lloyds, Midland, National Westminster etc. (and similar posts in building societies).

Salary range: from £12,500 (graduates) or £7,000 (non-grads) to £50,000+.

Qualifications: for graduate entry a 'good' degree, and you have to pass a battery of interviews, psychometric tests, and group exercises (how to cross a river using a bin liner and a pole . . .) Non-grads may or may not need some school grades, it depends on the bank. English and maths GCSEs always an advantage; there are fast-track opportunities for school-leavers.

Will suit you if you: are enthusiastic, energetic, able to work in a team; get a buzz from financial figures and computers; are persuasive.

Perks: depending on the bank, free banking, very low interest rates on mortgages and other loans; cash bonuses; excellent salary; regular hours.

Pitfalls: you're expected to be responsible about your own financial affairs. Won't suit you if you're highly independent/free-spirited.

Future opportunities: graduate recruitment has been known to be frozen periodically, but apply anyway and once you're in, the main banks all have good, organised career structures. You learn new skills rapidly and progress to branch manager, area manager . . . If you leave the bank you can use your financial skills to run your own business.

How to get in: • ring personnel in your local branches to ask for the right address to apply directly – there's usually an area office.

If you want an easy life, don't be a bank manager. Banks have become competitive and energetic. The chances of your success depend on your being motivated, and an ability to manage and make decisions within a team. It's a lot to do with marketing new accounts to people who suspect the new is no different from the old. And in today's climate there's a never-ending queue of business owners all knocking on your door for help – and cash.

As a trainee manager you'll probably start at a high street branch, doing everything from handing out money to customers at the counter to answering the phone to irate business account holders who want to know why they've been overcharged. In the refers department you might have, in your first year, the freedom to grant loans up to £1,000 – the first taste of power.

With on-going training and annual assessments, you'll pinpoint the area in which you'd like to specialise. You might end up travelling between different branches to coach new cashiers. You could, like one thirty-year-old woman, be sole manager of a small string of provincial branches. Or you could tiptoe into the soft-carpeted world of private banking, where you'll help to administrate the private estates of a small number of very wealthy customers, and discreetly advise them on how to minimise their taxes.

And in your early years you will be strongly encouraged by your employer to take the Chartered Institute of Bankers' exams, involving masses of home study. It's not an easy life – but it is a profitable one.

MAGAZINE SALES EXECUTIVE/ PUBLISHER

Working for: magazine publishing houses.

Salary range: sales execs – £9,000 basic to £30,000, plus sales bonuses; publishers – £25,000 to £60,000, more at director level.

Qualifications: some employers prefer you to have a degree, subject and college not important. The main thing is to be able to 'sell' yourself to the employer.

Will suit you if you: are motivated by money; have 'the barrow boy's ability to sell', to quote one director; enjoy the creative aspects of magazines; are a good manager of people, tenacious and persuasive.

Perks: car; lunching, wining and dining; some travel.

Pitfalls: if you can't sell your product, you're out. After a day or a week of no sales, you still have to pick up the phone and try again.

Future opportunities: the able and determined can flourish. The industry has been through sticky times but there are still thousands of magazines in the UK – you could end up publishing a business magazine, a women's magazine, or, eventually, buy your own string of publications. Or move into newspapers.

How to get in: • write to and ring the personnel departments of the big publishing companies and/or the advertising managers of magazines – get their numbers from *BRAD*, a directory, from libraries • read *Media Week* and *Campaign* for industry info and job ads; contact companies which are expanding.

Magazines could scarcely exist if it weren't for ads. As an advertising sales executive, it's up to you to sell space in your publication to advertisers.

You'll ring up likely manufacturers or media planners at agencies, to persuade them to promote their goods in your magazine. You'll cite market research that shows your readers are the perfect customers for a particular perfume, computer, or whatever. You'll quote a price from the magazine's rate card – say, £5,000 for a full-page colour ad – but are prepared to negotiate a discount.

Next step up is ad sales manager, then publisher, responsible for the financial livelihood of the magazine. Publishers come from a range of backgrounds, such as editorial and advertising. The essential thing is to understand the market, and how to increase sales or come up with other ways to make more money for your company.

Study all the magazines you can lay your hands on. See how they're put together, whether the identity of the magazine is coming across clearly. Then apply to the companies who publish them, armed with ideas about how you feel their sales could be improved.

As you get more senior, part of your job could be to hunt for new purchases: 'The greatest buzz is buying your first magazine for your company,' says one publishing director of twenty-eight. That could mean spending half a million or more.

PATENT AGENT

Working for: large industrial organisations, private patent agent firms, Government departments.

Salary range: £13,000 while training, then £20,000 to £40,000+; partners earn more.

Qualifications: you need a scientific or technical background, usually a science or engineering degree. You'll learn legal skills during training on the job: you study for the Chartered Institute of Patent Agents exams – it takes three to four years to qualify, and then there's a European Qualifying Examination to do.

Will suit you if you: are analytical, logical, an able and meticulous writer; have knowledge of other languages – French and German not essential but 'highly desirable' to read if not to speak, says The Chartered Institute of Patent Agents. Basically, you need to be a bit of a scientist, lawyer and linguist rolled into one.

Perks: seeing brand new innovations before the rest of the world does; being the one who ensures the inventors don't get ripped off by copycats.

Pitfalls: accuracy is everything in this job – get your facts wrong and an invention can be copied by all; the exams are a bit of a burden.

Future opportunities: some 76,000 patent, design, trademark and servicemark applications go to the Patent Office every year. Rise in a big industrial company, become a partner in a private practice, or run your own!

How to get in: • careers, courses and firms info from The Chartered Institute of Patent Agents, Staple Inn Buildings, High Holborn, London WC1V 7PZ, tel 071–405 9450 • read *Chartered Patent Agents*, a comprehensive Ivanhoe Guide to the profession, available in some libraries.

How much is an idea worth? If the idea is a brand new invention, like the first ever personal computer, or the first calorie-free cooking oil, then it's worth millions in terms of future sales. Patent agents are the ones who ensure good ideas, designs, and product names are legally recognised as the property of the people who thought them up. It involves finding the best legal form of protection, getting it registered with the Patent Office, and using legal means if necessary against people who try to produce the same thing, without permission from the patent holder.

You'll start as a technical assistant, or trainee, learning under the guidance of a registered patent agent. One of your clients might be a cosmetics company, who want to relaunch a range under a new name. It's your job to check with the Patent Office that the name hasn't been registered before, and then to register it as a trademark. Another company might bring into your office an amazing new type of sweet that changes colour as you look at it. You do searches through existing patents to check it's not been done before, and then register it, in the UK and abroad.

'If you enjoy science but pure research doesn't appeal, this is a good way of keeping in touch with new developments,' explains one trainee patent agent. 'And it's exciting when you see something really new.'

STOCKBROKER

Working for: one of the companies which buy and sell stocks and shares in the International Stock Exchange on behalf of banks and other financial institutions; some private individuals.

Salary range: some clerks start at £5,000 to £6,000, others at £8,000 to £10,000. Graduate trainees earn more; most established stockbrokers are on between £40,000 and £60,000, depending on the quantity of business passing through their hands . . . but the sky really is the limit.

Qualifications: none required but graduate recruitment is a big feature of many firms. You can get in after GCSEs or A Levels; others (especially researchers/analysts who are usually graduates, see below) switch from a first career in banking or similar.

Will suit you if you: have fast mental reflexes; can calculate figures instantaneously; are a clear communicator; have nerves of steel and stamina; are persuasive; have an extensive knowledge of current news, especially financial.

Perks: whopping great salaries for the lucky and able.

Pitfalls: burn-out in this stressful career – make a wrong judgment and you can lose millions for your clients; job cuts.

Future opportunities: • move into banking or other financial institutions or business or become a financial writer.

How to get in: • general info from The Stock Exchange, Clerks' Fund, Wingate House, Fore Street, London EC2Y 5EJ • apply to member firms, listed in *The Member Firms of the London Stock Exchange* or *Central London Yellow Pages* (in libraries) • read, listen to and watch financial news non-stop.

Brokers don't stand about on the floor of the Exchange shouting 'Buy!' 'Sell!' Most of the business goes on in the stockbroker firms' offices, by computer and phone. Since deregulation – the Big Bang – in 1986, stockbrokers now do one of three jobs:

You can be a researcher/analyst, investigating how well various public companies are doing and putting reports together recommending whether it's worth buying or selling their shares.

You can be a broker – which basically comes down to (though stockbrokers prefer not to see themselves like this) being an account executive. You court new clients, handle their accounts, and persuade them to buy or sell shares on the recommendations of your researchers.

Or you can be a market maker, the one who actually does the buying and selling, over the phone, at the best prices possible.

Stockbrokers earn their living by having a cut of all transactions, so the more transactions you make, and the bigger they are, the more money you make. And the more money you lose, the quicker you're out.

STORE MANAGER

Working for: department stores, supermarkets, retail chains and independent shops.

Salary range: varies widely according to the store's turnover, but broadly from £9,000 to £40,000; managing directors up to £60,000+.

Qualifications: the big chains have graduate trainee schemes (any degree subject though you can choose to do a degree in retailing), but you can get in just as easily after GCSEs or A Levels/BTEC diploma, and relevant experience as a sales assistant on the shop floor. You then get on-the-job training with some short courses provided by your store group.

Will suit you if you: have a good commercial nose, leadership qualities, and can work in a team; have excellent people skills; understand the principles of selling; are numerate, analytical, enthusiastic, open to new ideas and determined.

Perks: discounts on your store's products; car and other corporate trimmings.

Pitfalls: dealing with recessions, shop-lifting, and tough competition to get to your managerial position; also some Saturday and, increasingly, Sunday work.

Future opportunities: retail managerial skills are highly transferable: take them to another chain, or start your own shop or franchise.

How to get in: • apply to all the major stores • see job ads in quality papers • for industry info and jobs, read *Retail Week* and any trade magazines that apply to your area: e.g. *Drapers Record* for clothes shops.

Your first days as a management trainee won't be spent in a rarefied office atmosphere: you'll be on the shop floor, learning basic principles of retail management first hand – from ensuring the cash tills are manned (by you, probably) to seeing for yourself what tempts customers to buy.

As you go on you'll spend periods in every department, including personnel, where you might help to devise a new staff training scheme to increase levels of efficiency and politeness, and customer services – where you manage the cashiers and work out rotas so there are plenty of tills working during busy periods like lunchtimes and Saturdays.

With the help of short courses, you develop research and analytic skills, so you can introduce new ways of maximising sales per square metre of floor – strategies like placing chocolate next to the cash desk, and arranging for the scent of baking bread to waft across the store were devised by your predecessors. You will be expected to come up with new schemes, and the creative process of that, mixed with the pleasures of high profits for your shop, can be extremely satisfying. As is the promotion ladder when you get it right: all the way up to being the manager in charge of the store, with responsibility for some 500 staff and an annual turnover of up to £50 million.

VENTURE CAPITALIST

Working for: venture capital companies (many linked to banks); yourself.

Salary range: £15,000 to £100,000+, and bonuses, share schemes.

Qualifications: you'll be a chartered accountant, or have an MBA, or have suitable experience in banks, computing, or any other area of industry.

Will suit you if you: are commercially aware, numerate, analytical; have good people skills; are mature, willing to take calculated risks; enjoy helping new businesses.

Perks: seeing someone's great idea become a multi-million-pound concern, and knowing that you made it possible (and that you're a shareholder).

Pitfalls: losing your company's or your own money in a business that fails.

Future opportunities: you do as well as your fledgling businesses do.

How to get in: • contact individual companies such as this major one: 3i plc, 91 Waterloo Road, London SE1 8XP • further info from British Venture Capital Association, 3 Catherine Place, London SW1E 6DX, tel 071–233 5212 • see job ads in *Financial Times* and other quality papers.

A venture capitalist is a talent scout, of sorts. Your role is to find the future Anita Roddicks – people with the business flair to make it as entrepreneurs. You'll provide funds and/or give them specialised advice to get them up and running. If your protégés succeed, you get a share in their profits; if you're unlucky, they go bust, and you lose your investment. It's not like being a bank manager, because you don't simply lend the money, you invest it. And the risks are higher which makes it more fun.

You'll seek out some new businesses but, in practice, most would-be entrepreneurs come to you. You have to develop a fine commercial nose, an ability to judge, in the space of one or two meetings, whether your clients have the right temperament and abilities to succeed. When someone comes to you with a brand new invention which you can see is good, rather than downright crackpot, it's an exciting feeling. But you have to make sure that the company has the financial nous necessary to survive.

Amber Rudd, twenty-nine, runs her own venture capital business in London. She moved into it after a few years in banking, which she entered as a graduate. 'It's less of a risk business today than it was in the eighties,' she reckons. 'Big venture capital companies concentrate on relatively safe investment, like management buyouts, or expansions.'

Amber sees her role as mainly advisory, so she doesn't often put money into businesses, but advises them on the best sources of loans and grants. Sometimes she arranges a bank loan, or invests some of her company's funds. 'But more often, if people want £10,000 or so to get going, I advise them to go to their family and friends, because, especially in a bad financial climate, they are the ones who are most likely to take the risk.'

SOCIAL CONSCIENCE

Do you think a lot of people have an unfair deal? Do the pictures on TV, of children starving in East Africa, or riots breaking out in poor British neighbourhoods, make you want to do something *now*?

Luckily, there are good opportunities to turn anger into action. Charities have never been more effectively run. There are new alternative health occupations like aromatherapy and sports therapy. And the pillars of our community – the health service, legal system, police force and schools – want bright and caring people all the time.

In most of these careers you won't make your fortune, though you will earn enough for a decent living. But the real reward is knowing that you've done your best to improve the lives of others around you. And that improves your life too.

AROMATHERAPIST

Working for: your own practice or in an alternative health centre; some hospices and hospitals (if you have a medical background).

Salary: from £15 to £50 per session, up to around twenty-five sessions per week; with holidays £15,000 to £50,000+ annually. But you have to build up the business.

Qualifications: you should first get a diploma, from an ITEC course (for which you can get a grant) or a range of courses privately e.g. The Tisserand Institute which runs courses at the Royal Masonic Hospital in London (costs £2,500 for six months full-time; you need four GCSEs and have to pass an interview).

Will suit you if you: are a good carer, physically strong (massage requires muscles), reassuring, organised, self-reliant.

Perks: you can work anywhere; the tools of your trade are scented oils designed to make people feel good – some of it will rub off on you!

Pitfalls: little security; it's up to you do the marketing, advertising, and sheer hard work to make your business boom.

Future opportunities: glowing – this is a growing industry.

How to get in: • for ITEC course details send large SAE to ITEC, James House, Oakelbrook Mill, Newent, Glos GL18 1HD, tel (0531) 821875 • accredited courses info from Aromatherapy Organisations Council, 3 Latymer Close, Braybrooke, Market Harborough, Leicester LE16 8LN • prospectus from The Tisserand Institute, 65 Church Road, Hove, East Sussex BN3 2BD • see IMAGE CONSULTANT for loans info.

Aromatherapy is treatment with a range of essential plant oils, all of which have different beneficial effects on people's well-being – from bergamot for skin blemishes, to sensual ylang-ylang for mental tension. Many practitioners also have counselling skills.

Gail Neckel, twenty-eight, runs her own aromatherapy business after an earlier career in textiles and marketing. 'I was made redundant, so I used the pay-off to invest in a new direction. I'm really pleased that I did.'

Coming to aromatherapy from a previous career seems to be the ideal way to do it. Aromatherapists recommend that you read all you can about the subject in health books and magazines; ask around, talk to a practising aromatherapist if possible; then send off for all the prospectuses that interest you – go for something that appeals and is accredited (see above). The Tisserand course teaches massage, counselling, knowledge of fifty or so essential oils, reflexology (treating ailments in different parts of the body by massaging specific areas on the feet and hands), nutrition and business skills.

Gail first tried working in an alternative health centre, but found she was paying half her outgoings in rent. Today, like many aromatherapists, she works from home. It makes sense, as well as all the private clients, to get yourself some contracts – perhaps regular work at a local health farm or club, or become the aromatherapist for a particular sports team. There are also opportunities for part-time teaching.

BARRISTER

Working for: yourself, in a set of chambers alongside other barristers, for government or large businesses.

Salary range: as of recently, during pupillage you should now get £6,000 to £20,000, barristers from £30,000 upwards – £100,000 to £300,000 is common; Government salaries from £17,000 to £56,000.

Qualifications: a law degree followed by a year at Inns of Court School of Law (Bar school), followed by a year's pupillage (apprenticeship) at a set of chambers. Or any degree followed by a one-year conversion course, then Bar school etc. You'll almost certainly need a 2:1 or a first in your degree.

Will suit you if you: have an intelligent, analytical mind; can absorb information fast; can 'perform' in court; have very good people skills.

Perks: be your own boss and earn a fortune.

Pitfalls: after training and pupillage, you may fail to get a tenancy in a set. There are only around 7,000 barristers, and every year many hundreds more seek to join them; plus boring waiting periods when you're in court.

Future opportunities: barristers tend to stick to their chambers for life, but some switch; excellent opportunities in business.

How to get in: • shop around for a good university through the *UCCA Handbook*: the biggest percentage of newcomers is from the universities of London, Cambridge and Oxford • send A4 SAE with 58p stamp for careers info to The Bar Council, 3 Bedford Row, London WC1R 4DB.

'A practising barrister must promote and protect . . . his lay client's best interests and do so without regard to his own interests or to any consequences to himself or to any other person.' So runs the code of conduct of the Bar.

The principles may have stayed the same for centuries, but the last five years has seen a real shaking up of the system by which you become a barrister. To see if you like the career, you can go and do a mini-pupillage – what other industries would call work experience – at chambers. At Bar school, there's more emphasis on developing people skills.

Sets of chambers are basically groups of practising barristers who pool their office resources. Aspiring barristers, while at Bar school, apply to a number of chambers . . . you'll probably write to eighty or so, and accept whatever you're offered. Chambers specialise in different areas of law: criminal or civil, property, family, patents, and so on.

Barristers are given new cases by the barrister's clerk in their set. The clerk is, in effect, an agent. Clerks cultivate new business from solicitors; therefore, barristers do well to get on with the clerk, to get work. As a barrister, you scarcely talk to your client, but simply represent his or her interests in the court. That can mean getting a sheaf of papers on Monday from a solicitor for a court appearance on Tuesday. You have to absorb facts fast. But you can take time off when you choose.

BUYER FOR ECO-FRIENDLY GOODS

Working for: charities that sell third-world goods, such as Oxfam, Friends of the Earth; eco-friendly businesses.

Salary: assistants from £12,000; buyers/managers £17,000–£28,000+.

Qualifications: some employers ask for graduates (degree subject not important), otherwise, some experience of retailing, mail-order catalogues, management, charity work. Should also understand green issues.

Will suit you if you: have an eye for good quality; have negotiating acumen; can handle budgets; have prior experience in a related charity or retailing.

Perks: depending on the organisation, there could be travel; dealing in beautiful hand-crafted items; helping other economies.

Pitfalls: buying a consignment that doesn't match your organisation's strict principles; too much travel can mean relationships suffer.

Future opportunities: the mix of business and conscience makes this a long-term growth area with promising career opportunities: supermarkets such as Asda, BHS and Tesco are already selling eco-friendly clothing.

How to get in: see job ads in the *Guardian* on Wednesdays • for general info send large SAE to Friends of the Earth, 26-28 Underwood Street, London N1 7JQ – write to Martin Jones re. volunteer work • for jobs info, send large SAE to Personnel Department, Oxfam, 274 Banbury Road, Oxford OX2 7DZ • if you have some experience of full-time work, contact Charity Recruitment, 40 Rosebery Ave, London EC1R 4RN, tel 071-833 0770 9.30 a.m. – 5.30 p.m.

This is your chance to shop till you drop – and know it's in a good cause. Sarah Tyack, twenty-four, is trading assistant at Friends of the Earth, helping to produce their ever-growing catalogue of unbleached cotton clothes, gifts and other goodies.

Her route in was fairly typical: 'I got in initially by applying to be a general volunteer. Then, when a suitable job came up, I had the right experience and was taken on.' Charities take on many volunteers, who get their expenses paid. As a volunteer, you won't get preferential treatment for a job . . . but it helps.

The next stage up is buyer or trading manager. It varies from place to place, but managers tend to be office-based, buyers travel more. To get these posts you either train up from your junior position in the charity, or clock up experience in commercial retailing then switch. In the office, you'll commission designers to make new lines, and place bulk orders with merchandise suppliers. You'll spend a lot of your time on the phone, in meetings, on factory visits. You meet new suppliers by attending trade fairs regularly.

Buyers, like those at Oxfam, travel out to India, Asia, Peru, East Africa to buy goods direct. 'You're likely to be in your mid-twenties onwards, with craft retail experience and understanding of management and design,' says Andrew Simms from Oxfam head office. 'A taste for adventure also helps!'

DENTIST

Working for: yourself, often with one or more partners, in a dental clinic; hospitals; Armed Forces; large companies; teaching in universities.

Salary range: £18,000 to £50,000+.

Qualifications: dental school requirements vary (information from the address below). Typically you need three A Levels or the equivalent. Some of these can be non-sciences. The dental course lasts five years and combines theoretical and practical training – course subjects include anatomy, biochemistry, dental materials science. Dentists update their skills regularly throughout their careers.

Will suit you if you: like the subject; have a reassuring, sympathetic manner; are a hard worker; enthusiastic; can handle business admin.

Perks: being your own boss; seeing a patient transformed after complicated treatment.

Pitfalls: irregular income; no security; phobic patients.

Future opportunities: good. Always a need for dentists and the new emphasis on prevention, plus new technology, makes it a dynamic profession.

How to get in: • career and courses info (A4 SAE preferred) from The General Dental Council, 37 Wimpole Street, London W1M 8DQ, tel 071–486 2171.

Killer dentists, maniacs with dripping syringes . . . the film industry has a lot to answer for when it comes to our image of the average dentist . . .

But the reality is better than ever, thanks to enormous advances in the technology and psychology of dental care. The trend today is to make surgeries look welcoming and comfortable as well as efficient. Today the younger dentists don't brandish needles very often, though there always is a need for fillings, bridges, crowns and the like. The emphasis now is on preventive health care.

Says one dentist, 'My particular interest is gum disease and the whole practice is run along preventive lines.

'Hygienists work with me three days a week and we concentrate on scaling, cleaning, giving oral hygiene instruction and generally motivating the patients to look after their own health. I actually spend more time talking than doing!'

You will probably go into an established general practice after qualifying, then, a year or so later, you'll become a partner of the practice or buy and run your own, which will involve hiring staff. The investment either way is pretty big: the onus is on you to build up your business into a flourishing one, to pay off the mortgage and prosper.

DOCTOR

Working for: initially the National Health Service; then possibly the private sector; Armed Forces.

Salary range: £12,000 to £45,000; the sky's the limit in the private sector.

Qualifications: you need three good A Levels in chemistry, physics, biology or similar, plus good GCSEs; it has been known for people with A Levels in the arts to get into medical school. Then a two-year pre-clinical course, followed by three-year clinical course in hospital, learning in the wards and attending lectures on all aspects of medical practice. Then, one year pre-registration as a house officer in a general hospital. After five plus one years, you're registered with the General Medical Council.

Perks: saving the lives of many people; improving those of others.

Pitfalls: the year of hell, the pre-registration year, during which you're working night and day (but the hours have improved lately); GPs in particular are often very overworked; the stress of patients dying prematurely.

Future opportunities: one of the most valuable skills to have, always in high demand: you can have a flourishing career specialising in general practice, brain surgery . . . or go abroad as a relief and development worker.

How to get in: • send A5 SAE for careers and courses info/specific queries to the Information Officer, British Medical Association, BMA House, Tavistock Square, London WC1H 9JP, tel 071-387-4499; or call in at the Enquiries office between 9 a.m. and 5 p.m., Monday to Friday.

It's tough to get into medical school: in one recently quoted example, of 2,000 applications to a London hospital, 100 were offered places. It's gruelling when you're training to become a doctor and being one is not easy either.

After qualifying at the end of the clinical course, you apply to hospitals throughout the land as a house officer, your pre-registration year. From day one you have to make decisions that could determine a patient's life or death.

One house doctor describes her first experience, in casualty: 'You're in charge of admitting the new cases, and you don't know what's going to come in next.' It could mean receiving a warning that an ambulance is on its way. You're told it's a car crash victim. You organise nurses, equipment, anything else you think you might need. The ambulance arrives; the casualty is a young boy. You do essential checks on him even as he's being wheeled into the Accident and Emergency ward. You call specialist consultants as they're required, and hand over the boy into the charge of the one who has to give priority attention. The boy probably won't live, but you don't have time to think about it now, because in another bed behind closed curtains, there's someone else who needs your attention . . . fast.

Once you're registered, you can choose to specialise in one of a wide number of areas such as general or private practice, surgery, psychiatry or research. There are good financial rewards later in your career, but given the accompanying stresses, there is no way you can be a doctor unless it's a strongly held vocation. And, of course, for many it is.

LEGAL SECRETARY/LEGAL EXECUTIVE

Working for: solicitors in private practices; Government or big business.

Salary range: secretaries £12,000 to £19,000; executives £17,000 to £35,000.

Qualifications: secretary – typing skills (60 wpm); shorthand not so important because most solicitors today dictate into tape recorders; you may require four GCSEs. Legal executive – four GCSEs grades A–C including English. To become a legal executive you study either at a local college or by correspondence course for Institute of Legal Executive exams. These exams usually take four years part-time; you work while you learn.

Will suit you if you: are organised and hard-working; can absorb information quickly; can turn legal jargon into plain English; have a good phone manner; are diplomatic and determined.

Perks: good prospects; varied work.

Pitfalls: you must push your own career forward: many firms may think they're supporting you in your ambition, but they're so busy they forget to give you on-the-job training.

How to get in: • jobs for both at recruitment agencies • contact The Institute of Paralegal Training, The Mill, Clymping Street, Clymping, Littlehampton, West Sussex BN17 5RN • contact The Institute of Legal Executives, Kempston Manor, Kempston, Bedford MK42 7AB, tel (0234) 841000.

The wonderful thing about law as a career is that it's open to all: you can go from being a junior secretary to a fully fledged solicitor in three easy (all right, not that easy) steps. Or, if you prefer, you can stay a legal secretary, or stick at the middle rung and remain a legal executive.

This is how the system works: you can join a firm of solicitors as a legal secretary (there are secretarial courses that carry a legal element e.g. London Chamber of Commerce and Industry, which could tip the balance when it comes to getting a job). Or, if you have the GCSEs (some have A Levels) you can join as a trainee legal executive, although currently this is harder to do. Secretaries and trainees then train in exactly the same way, going to a local college in the evenings or by correspondence course, learning how to do their boss's job.

As a legal secretary, you do a lot of fielding of phone calls, typing letters and contracts, and filing. Once you've made it to executive, you're all but a solicitor. Clients come to you to discuss matrimonial problems, house moves, wills. You advise people accused of petty crimes, and you draw up legal contracts.

Recruitment agents for both jobs say that there are more openings in City work than high-street firms, especially in litigation, where you'd be processing law suits for commercial companies.

NURSE

Working for: local health authority hospitals, private hospitals, clinics, general practices, agencies; the community as a nurse or midwife.

Salary range: £6,820–£7,900 basic (Project 2000 trainees – a new programme with more emphasis on preventive health care – start on approximately £4,500). Qualified nurses – £10,820–£44,000. You get extra for working unsocial hours, and approximately £2,000 more annually if you work in London.

Qualifications: to become a registered general nurse, five GCSEs or equivalent, grades A–C (to train as a midwife, these must include English language and one science). You have to be at least sixteen and a half to apply and at least seventeen and a half at start of training. From October 1993, applications in England are being processed through a central clearing house between 1 October and 31 December annually, to start training in summer or autumn of the following year – further information about all UK countries from ENB, address below.

Will suit you if you: are self-reliant and can use your initiative; are able to work well in a team, are physically fit and not squeamish; can communicate well, listen, come up with imaginative solutions and plan budgets.

Perks: the satisfaction of seeing a patient transformed into a happy, well person; overtime allowances; gifts and cards from grateful patients.

Pitfalls: the trauma of a patient dying; working irregular hours; relatively low pay.

Future opportunities: it's extremely tough to get a first job after qualifying; but agency work is generally available, and jobs abroad. Later: management.

How to get in: • careers and general info from English National Board for Nursing, Midwifery and Health Visiting – contact ENB Careers, PO Box 356, Sheffield S8 0SJ, tel (0742) 555012, 10 a.m.–4 p.m. • see job ads in *Nursing Times*.

'One in five nurses seeks job abroad,' screamed a newspaper headline recently. Nursing is not the simple career option it used to be; health service cutbacks mean that newly qualified nurses find it hard to get their first staff job. A report published in 1992 by the Institute of Manpower Studies showed that in two years 8,000 nurses have left the UK intending to find work abroad. Most nurses you see in a hospital ward, talking to patients, administering pills, injections, reporting on patients' progress to doctors, are students, with uncertain futures.

But there is agency work about – you register with an agency and temp at different hospitals, even posh private clinics. And there are jobs abroad if you're tempted to travel. You can train further as a midwife, then pack your skills in your suitcase, and go . . . (see also RELIEF AND DEVELOPMENT WORKER).

'Once you've got your first job in the health service you should be OK as far as getting future jobs is concerned,' says an adviser at the Royal College of Nursing. You could also find work as a community nurse, helping people to take part in their own health care, at home. A rewarding career, but for the truly dedicated only.

NURSERY NURSE

Working for: nurseries, crèches, schools, families, hospitals.
Salary: £7,000 to £14,000.
Qualifications: required by many employers and, in any case, highly useful. Principal course is the NNEB (National Nursery Examination Board) certificate at local colleges, during which you get placement in most of the above work areas. It lasts two or more years, can be done part-time, and is heavily subscribed so apply early. Combination of practical lessons and theory: including health, English, environment studies, learning why families and society are the way they are. Some colleges ask for GCSEs.
Will suit you if you: like children; are responsible, caring, patient, mature, friendly, level-headed and creative; have staying power.
Perks: watching young children develop and achieve things you've taught them.
Pitfalls: when one baby falls ill, they all fall ill; some tricky parents.
Future opportunities: a baby-booming market, as more nurseries start up to fill the real demand from working mothers; run your own.
How to get in: • for careers and courses info: The National Nursery Examination Board, 8 Chequer Street, St Albans, Herts AL1 3XZ, tel (0727) 47636 • see job ads in *The Lady* and *Nursery World*, local papers, word of mouth • your college will have contacts with local nurseries.

At the start of the nursery nurse's day, some sixteen or so children turn up, aged three months to four. You and your colleagues will supervise different groups. You might be the nursery nurse in charge of, say, seven babies, which means you do everything seven times: feed seven babies, give seven drinks, change seven nappies, play with and read to seven babies, give seven lunches, change seven more nappies, tuck seven babies up in bed, play some more with seven babies . . . on fine days, you'll take two babies out for a walk in the tandem buggy.

Lucy McDonell, nineteen, works at Clifton Tots Day Nursery in Bristol. 'You need to keep coming up with new ideas to keep them entertained,' she says. She believes it helps, whether you're applying to college or for a job, to be able to say you've had experience with children: baby-sitting, childcare options at school. Her employer, Marcella Cunningham, adds that successful job candidates show ability, enthusiasm and the right attitude.

Older children need different sorts of stimuli: at Lucy's nursery, a teddy-bear's picnic was held. The children gave out invitations to the babies, planned places and party decorations every day for a week. They gained a sense of planning and responsibility, while having fun.

And that's the crux of it. Young children can't help but learn from everything they see and do. It's up to you to give them positive images. As the NNEB puts it, 'The early years of childhood are those during which young children go through their most rapid period of development – physically, socially, emotionally and intellectually.' She may have a traditionally humble status, but the nursery nurse is in an influential position.

NUTRITIONIST/ DIETITIAN

Working for: research institutions, NHS, food manufacturers, supermarkets, food promotion bodies and pressure groups.

Salary range: £14,000 to £40,000.

Qualifications: a degree in nutrition (three years) or nutrition and dietetics (four and a half years); there are also post-grad dietetics courses. Good courses are found at the University of Surrey, and King's College, London.

Will suit you if you: have an enquiring mind; are interested in food; care about people's well-being; are numerate, good at communicating, and realistic.

Perks: flexible hours; making people well through diet.

Pitfalls: nutrition is a fairly new science and hence not recognised everywhere. You need the dietetics element to be accepted by many employers, including the NHS. Catch 22: supermarkets etc. only require nutrition training, but they're looking for people with experience, and you can't get the experience without the dietetics element.

Future opportunities: expanding. The British Dietetic Association circulates a vacancies list to its members. You could travel as a RELIEF AND DEVELOPMENT WORKER, move into nutrition journalism or be a freelance consultant.

How to get in: • send standard SAE for careers info to The British Dietetic Association, 7th Floor, Elizabeth House, 22 Suffolk Street Queensway, Birmingham B1 1LS, tel 021–643 5483.

Here's one example of nutritionists at work. Recent studies by nutritionists at the Scottish Agricultural College, Ayr, found that our dietary levels of the mineral selenium – derived from the soil in which our crops and vegetables grow – have halved since 1978. The culprits appear to be fertilizers, metal pollution, acid rain and over-processing of foods. Low selenium levels have been linked in some cases to increased risk of cancer and heart disease (this doesn't mean we're all going to fall prey to one of those conditions). The research means that nutritionists may recommend eating more vegetables, plus supplements, to susceptible people.

As a nutritionist, you analyse people's diets to see how much of each nutrient they receive. You may do it on a large scale for research purposes – like the example given above – or for individuals. The NHS dietitian is an example of the latter: you spend about 80 per cent of your time talking to people, discussing their diets and suggesting realistic amendments.

In a food producing company, or a supermarket, you will work alongside the food scientist. You work out how much fat, sugar, carbohydrates, minerals and vitamins are in each food, and check that processing and packaging methods don't strip it of selenium and all the other minerals. You write the nutritional labels that the rest of us study before we buy.

OCCUPATIONAL PSYCHOLOGIST

Working for: large commercial companies; Civil Service and other Government bodies; yourself as an independent consultant.

Salary range: £12,000 to £40,000+; for consultants, the sky's the limit.

Qualifications: a degree in psychology or occupational psychology, followed usually by an MSc (if you have it you qualify to be a Chartered Psychologist); good universities include Birkbeck College, London, Hull, Nottingham, Sheffield.

Will suit you if you: care about people and are curious about what motivates them; are keen to improve working conditions, an accurate researcher and statistician; understand business.

Perks: bonuses, health schemes and all the corporate extras of big business; if self-employed, the freedom to choose your hours.

Pitfalls: employers who think a quick psychometric test is a foolproof way of judging a candidate's aptitude for a job – but no test is 100 per cent accurate.

Future opportunities: a growth industry, especially in the area of independent consultancy; you could become a CAREERS COUNSELLOR.

How to get in: • for careers and courses info send a large SAE to The British Psychological Society, St Andrews House, 48 Princess Road East, Leicester LE1 7DR (members of the Society regularly receive Appointments Memorandum – best source of job vacancies).

'I have to ensure that line managers always attempt to fill vacancies with people who are potentially better than the people they are replacing. I know this is common sense but it is not common practice,' says one occupational psychologist in a large manufacturing company.

It may be that the manager doesn't have time to search for the right person, and makes do with the nearest to hand. Or it may be that they prefer to have staff who are less bright than themselves and who won't, therefore, threaten them.

All of human life is in the workplace, and employees bring their personal insecurities to work alongside the sandwiches in their briefcases. As occupational psychologist (you may be called personnel or human resources manager) it's up to you to ensure that suitable staff are selected. That means staff with the right technical skills and the right personality to get on with the existing team. You'll give candidates tests, and interview them before passing the best on to the appointing manager.

You'll also look at any environmental improvements that can be made, and when necessary you turn troubleshooter. If a department has an unusually high staff turnover, you'll try to find out why, by looking at the pattern of staff appointments and absences, and talking to people in the department. Such problems often come down to a single bad manager, for whom you can then recommend whatever training and/or counselling may be required.

OPTICIAN: DISPENSING AND OPHTHALMIC

Working for: small private practices, and those owned by large groups; hospital eye departments.

Salary: dispensing – £12,000 to £22,000; ophthalmic – £18,000 to £30,000; franchise or business owners up to £80,000+.

Qualifications: for dispensing, you have three choices: join a practice and train by block release, or by an approved correspondence course, or do a two-year full-time course at college followed by one-year's practical experience. You need five GCSEs grades A–C or equivalent, to include English language or literature, maths or physics and another science. To be an ophthalmic optician you need two or three science A Levels, followed by a degree course at one of six universities/colleges (they're all equally well-considered), then one year's clinical experience in a practice.

Will suit you if you: are interested in physics, maths and the application of new scientific developments; care about people's well-being; are a good communicator; have sales skills and a sense of style; good business sense.

Perks: running your own business; seeing how a well-prescribed pair of contact lenses or glasses can transform someone's confidence and style.

Pitfalls: competition for ophthalmic places at college is currently tough; if you don't draw in the customers you're in trouble.

Future opportunities: equally good for dispensing and ophthalmic.

As a dispensing optician you can choose to train further to become an ophthalmic one, and be in an even better position for running your own practice.

How to get in: • careers and courses info from The British College of Optometrists, 10 Knaresborough Place, London SW5 0TG, tel 071–373 7765 • ditto from Association of British Dispensing Opticians, 6 Hurlingham Business Park, Sulivan Road, London SW6 3DU, tel 071–736 0088 • see job ads and industry info in *Optician* and *Dispensing Optics*.

The ophthalmic optician, also known as an optometrist, is the one who examines patients' eyes using an array of medical instruments, and issues a prescription. The dispensing optician helps patients choose glasses and contact lenses, and sells them. The two work together in one practice, and sometimes one is trained to do both jobs. The training to become an optometrist is more demanding, but can lead to some of the best rewards, not just financial. Illnesses like diabetes, hypertension and anaemia are first visible in the back of the retina, so as an ophthalmic optician you could refer your patients to their doctors when an illness is still in its early stages.

The best thing to do is to ask local opticians what it's like to get in and on in the two careers, and perhaps do a bit of work experience.

PHYSIOTHERAPIST

Working for: NHS in hospitals and in the community; schools; large companies; sports clinics, voluntary organisations; yourself.

Salary range: £11,500 to £28,500; self-employed from £55 to £81 per three-hour session.

Qualifications: you must do a three- to four-year degree course in physiotherapy validated by the Chartered Society of Physiotherapy (see below). Entrance requirements usually include three A Levels or equivalent, one of which is a biological science. Subjects you study include anatomy, physiology, behavioural sciences and the theory of physiotherapy skills. Work is mostly in college, with periods of direct patient care in a range of settings, under the supervision of experienced physiotherapists.

Will suit you if you: are good at communicating and caring; can work in a team; are physically fit, tolerant, happy to use own initiative; can motivate patients.

Perks: seeing one of your patients able to walk for the first time after a car crash; being your own boss.

Pitfalls: a very physically demanding job.

Future opportunities: move into research; teach; become self-employed or a SPORTS THERAPIST.

How to get in: • send A4 SAE for careers and courses info to Chartered Society of Physiotherapy, 14 Bedford Row, London WC1R 4ED, 071-242 1941, 2.30–4.30 p.m.

Here are just some of the things you could be doing a few years from now, if you were to train as a physiotherapist . . .

You're in the intensive care ward of a hospital, manipulating the limbs of an unconscious patient to keep them in good condition and ready to move again . . . You're at a local health centre, taking twenty pregnant women through antenatal exercises . . . You're at a sports clinic, massaging the limbs of an athlete and showing him exercises to strengthen weak muscles . . . It's the first half of a Premier League football match; Gazza, back from Italy, has just been kicked in the knee and you're running out to give some immediate treatment . . .

The chartered physiotherapist has a wide range of career options, but all involve helping people to have healthy, pain-free movement in their bodies. In fact, some of the things you may choose to do may equally be done by a sports therapist – the football physio, for example, doesn't necessarily have a physiotherapist's training.

But a physiotherapist's qualification can get you into many posts that wouldn't otherwise be open to you, from all jobs in the NHS, to some private health centres. It tends to make career progress easier.

POLICE DETECTIVE

Working for: one of the regional forces in England and Wales; Police Service in Scotland; Royal Ulster Constabulary in Northern Ireland.

Salary range: constables (everyone starts as a constable) – £11,790 to £19,674; other ranks – £18,819 to £39,360 (chief superintendents).

Qualifications: these vary from force to force, but generally you must be at least eighteen and a half when appointed and take a Standardised Entrance Test though you may be exempt if you have four GCSEs grades A–C, including English and maths; for graduate Accelerated Promotion Scheme you need a degree and to be under thirty; you must pass a medical and have reasonable eyesight; any height.

Will suit you if you: have a sense of values, courage, intelligence; are flexible; can cope with the unexpected.

Perks: free or subsidised accommodation; free uniform and equipment; as long as you've done twenty-five years' service you can retire at fifty on an annual pension equalling half your pensionable salary.

Pitfalls: dealing with armed and dangerous criminals; long slogging research; the frustration of not being able to close a case and having the criminal get away.

Future opportunities: it's competitive to get in at the moment (helps if you've done relevant work experience/voluntary work), but if you succeed there's a good career structure. Or you could become a private detective.

How to get in: • contact the Recruiting Officer at the nearest force headquarters, or write to the Chief Officer at the same address • for further info: Police Department, Room 516 Home Office, Queen Anne's Gate, London SW1H 9AT • Police Division, Scottish Office, St Andrew's House, Edinburgh E1H 3DE • Royal Ulster Constabulary, Brooklyn, Knock Road, Belfast BT5 6LE.

Move over, Inspector Morse. There's a dynamic new breed of police detectives who can solve crimes without being crabby.

Take Detective Inspector Karen Young, thirty-three, who tracked down the thief who stole records of Paddy Ashdown's affair from his solicitor's office during the last general election campaign. By combining a clue in a tabloid newspaper with her trawl through computer records, she located a man with the right name and background. The evidence stood up, and he was convicted.

That story sums up what you need to be a successful police detective today: the willingness to search for hours or days through tedious records, combined with quick, intuitive flashes of inspiration and lateral thinking.

You'll begin your career the way they all have to – as a constable in your local force, doing two years on the streets. The next step is to become a trainee investigator in your divisional crime squad. Then you need to pass a selection board to become a detective constable in CID, swapping your uniform for the civilian clothes of an undercover cop. Your promotion path is the same as any other branch of the force: sergeant, inspector and so on. Exciting, demanding, tough, and rewarding . . .

SOCIAL WORKER

Working for: local authorities, voluntary organisations, private companies and organisations.

Salary range: £11,000 to £25,000; up to £67,000 for directors.

Qualifications: you can get in without any, but to get on, you need a qualification awarded by the governing body, CCETSW (see below). Two of the three currently on offer are being phased out leaving just the Diploma in Social Work – a two-year course with work placements, which you can combine with a degree or masters. Two to three A Levels or similar to begin.

Will suit you if you: are emotionally stable, caring; mature, a good judge of people and problems, objective, practical, organised, a teamworker; have excellent people skills; are able to build a rapport with your clients.

Perks: satisfaction of seeing how you've helped people to rebuild their lives; you can work anywhere in the UK (or go abroad).

Pitfalls: lack of resources, bad management or wrong decisions in your team can lead to human misery . . . with you on the front page of the tabloids.

Future opportunities: many jobs being advertised – an increasing number of workplaces, from TV stations to factories. Or you could move into COUNSELLING.

How to get in: • contact the Central Council for Education and Training in Social Work: CCETSW Information Service, Derbyshire House, St Chad's Street, London WC1H 8AD, tel 071-278 2455 9 a.m.–5 p.m.; CCETSW Information Service, 6 Malone Road, Belfast BT9 5BN, tel (0232) 665390; CCETSW Information Service, 78/80 George Street, Edinburgh EH2 3BU, 031–220 0093 9.30 a.m.–1.30 p.m.; CCETSW Information Service, 2nd Floor, South Gate House, Wood Street, Cardiff CF1 1EW, tel (0222) 226257 • info on NVQs (learn on the job) from Joint Awarding Bodies office, c/o Division 22, City & Guilds of London Institute, 46 Britannia Street, London WC1X 9RG.

'Social workers try to help people with their personal, social and environmental problems and to live fuller, happier lives,' says the Central Council for Education and Training in Social Work. 'Social work can be bloody hard work,' says one social worker aged thirty. 'It can be an uphill struggle to help people who don't always want to help themselves.'

The trouble is, when clients are immersed in long-term problems – like a woman being battered by her partner, or a man who, abused as a child, has continued the pattern of abuse in his own young family – these become almost normal for them, an ingrained part of their lives. Any change is invariably unsettling: half-welcomed but half-feared.

So your role as a social worker is to talk and listen for long, patient sessions. Your clients may come to you for interviews in the social services department/your office, or you may visit them. You build up your clients' confidence and plan the best solutions, often practical: you arrange financial aid, better housing. And because hearing deep-seated problems all day long is stressful, it's important that you have support from your colleagues, and your own network of family and friends.

SOLICITOR

Working for: yourself in a practice, often with other partners; local or central government; the Magistrates' Courts Service; large businesses.

Salary range: £13,000 to £28,000 to start (depending on region); then up to £100,000 salaried; the sky's the limit for partners.

Qualifications: three routes in: three out of four solicitors-in-the-making do a law degree approved by the Law Society; or you can do another degree followed by a one- to two-year course covering the core law subjects – you need good A Levels in any subjects – ask advice of the universities you're targeting. Before being let loose on the high street, you do a legal practice course, then two years on a training contract (what used to be called 'Articles'), working for a firm. Or, do it without a degree, taking the LEGAL EXECUTIVE route.

Will suit you if you: have a good memory and a chess player's ability to plot the long-term consequences of a particular step; can absorb and process information fast; are a problem-solver, sympathetic and articulate.

Perks: being your own boss; opportunities to work abroad.

Pitfalls: it's currently difficult to get that first training contract with a firm; there have been redundancies; pricey to start your own practice.

Future opportunities: as our laws become more complex and more interconnected with the rest of Europe's, there's a growing demand for experts who can lead us through the legal maze.

How to get in: • contact The Law Society, Careers Office, 227/228 Strand, London WC2R 1BA, tel 071-242 1222.

What do solicitors actually do? The Law Society says a recent survey shows that your average solicitor spends 60 per cent of their time sorting out the legal complexities of commercial property, residential conveyancing, and general business – each in equal quantities. Matrimonial disputes take up less than 10 per cent of the day.

As a newly qualified solicitor you might go into a high street general practice, or head for the City and specialise in commercial litigation (helping businesses to sue others who've stolen their ideas). You could concentrate on acting for people accused of crimes, or be one of the many taking up local government posts.

Whichever area you choose, what you actually do boils down to solving problems. These are some of the problems you will encounter in a typical week: how to get compensation for someone who was hit by a motorbike; drawing up a watertight will; investing money bequeathed in a will; arranging a divorce; checking a company's documents for potential libel.

Clients will variously come and see you by appointment, or ring and discuss their business over the phone. Legal documents will be drawn up, and these take up a good deal of time; but you'll have staff: a LEGAL SECRETARY or LEGAL EXECUTIVE to do the routine work.

SPEECH/LANGUAGE THERAPIST

Working for: NHS in hospitals, health centres, adult training centres; schools; private practices.

Salary range: £11,718 to £30,000.

Qualifications: you need a degree: at least two A Levels and five GCSEs grades A–C or the equivalent to begin training at a college or university; most places require three A Levels including English, biology, or other specific subjects. You can do a three- or four-year degree in speech and language therapy or similar, or a two-year post-grad course. You'll study psychology, anatomy and physiology, the science of sound and language, and how to diagnose and treat speech and language disorders.

Will suit you if you: are caring; can get on well with a wide range of people; can inspire in patients confidence and belief in their own recovery; have a great liking for language and communication.

Perks: the sheer pleasure of hearing someone with brain damage speak for the first time – and witnessing the way such treatment can transform lives.

Pitfalls: frustration when progress is slow . . . or when treatment doesn't work.

Future opportunities: jobs are available throughout the UK. You can choose to specialise, rise up to a managerial role in the NHS, or work as a self-employed consultant and choose your own hours.

How to get in: send A5 SAE for careers and courses info to the accrediting body, the College of Speech and Language Therapists, 7 Bath Place, Rivington Street, London EC2A 3DR, tel 071-613 3855, 9 a.m.–4 p.m.

Sometimes, the person you're treating is not the person who has come to you with a speech problem, but that person's worried relatives: a four-year-old child has a tendency to stutter. His parents bring him in to the local health centre. You draw the child out, and can tell that he has no more than a normal degree of hesitation in speech, which could become worse if his parents start inhibiting him. So you reassure them, and show them how not to make too great a thing of any occasional stutters.

The next appointment is a teacher, who loses her voice by the end of every working week. You teach her some relaxation exercises that will ensure that instead of pushing the air out of her lungs like a fist that strikes and bruises the vocal chords, she does so more smoothly and naturally.

Next comes a high-flying business woman who had a car crash resulting in some brain damage which affects her speech. Through painstaking weekly exercises her speech is improving, and will soon be up to normal speed.

Talking clearly and effectively is something most people take for granted, but speech problems can make sufferers feel alienated from society. So as a speech and language therapist, along with curing voice problems, you're helping your patients/clients to feel happier and more confident social beings.

SPORTS THERAPIST

Working for: health clubs; sports centres; yourself.

Salary range: £10,000 (or less) to £35,000.

Qualifications: you need a knowledge of sport, physics and anatomy/biology. There are a few good courses you can take, including the International Health and Sports Therapy Diploma (see addresses below). Many switch from a related career e.g. PHYSIOTHERAPY, or from a first career in sports, or sports teaching.

Will suit you if you: have an active interest and understanding of sport; are physically fit and strong; care for people's well-being; are a good communicator with a reassuring manner, mature; have a good business sense.

Perks: be your own boss; have a well-toned body; manipulate the muscles of sports stars.

Pitfalls: difficult to win clients unless you have the contacts.

Future opportunities: interest in fitness is booming; with effective marketing and the right positive attitude you can build up your business.

How to get in: • send SAE to The International Institute of Sports Therapy, 109 Felpham Road, Felpham, West Sussex, PO22 7PW • send SAE to The Sports Council, 16 Upper Woburn Place, London WC1H 0QP, tel 071-388 1277 • be active in sports yourself: many clients come through word of mouth.

'A lot of people advertise sports therapy courses, most of which are only recognised by the people advertising them,' says a spokesperson at the Sports Council, pithily.

Sports therapy is a new discipline, and one with huge potential, since it appeals not only to sports people, but to non-sporting people too. But because it's new and in its early years, there's an element of anything goes. So it's best to stick to members' organisations like The International Institute of Sports Therapy which the Sports Council is happy to recommend.

Sports therapy combines the principles of massage – its major element – with exercise and sometimes an element of nutrition. 'A lot of what I do comes down to body realignment,' says Pat Liggett who was a speed skater before she became a sports therapist. 'Golf and cycling are examples of activities which mainly use one half of your body: in golf you swing the upper torso and arms; in cycling you have the piston motion of your legs. My role is to restore the muscle balance, through massage and exercises.' Similar principles could be applied in the case of a more sedentary person with back problems or shoulder stiffness caused by sitting at a desk for too long.

As a sports therapist, your ideal is to get a regular contract with a sports centre or health farm, and have private clients too. It's also good for your cv to be the therapist for a national sport team. Unfortunately, the amateur ones can't always afford to pay you.

TEACHER

Working for: primary and secondary schools, state and private sectors.

Salary range: £11,000 to £45,000+, plus some extra allowances.

Qualifications: for the private sector you need a good degree in the subject you wish to teach. In the state sector you need an educational qualification – either a four-year BEd degree or BA/BSc QTS (with Qualified Teacher Status), or a three-year general degree plus a one-year postgraduate certificate of education (PGCE). (In some cases, you don't need a degree.)

Will suit you if you: want wholeheartedly to teach; are a good communicator; are creative; have a sense of humour; can keep an unruly class in order.

Perks: long holidays, short teaching hours.

Pitfalls: masses of homework to mark in the evenings; extra-curricular activities and other duties.

Future opportunities: the number of primary school pupils has been rising, and will do so till the year 2000, so there's always a demand for teachers (there are over 400,000 teachers in state schools). You could teach children with special needs, or work abroad (see RELIEF AND DEVELOPMENT WORKER).

How to get in: • abundant careers and courses info from TASC Publicity Unit, Elizabeth House, York Road, London SE1 7PH, tel 071-925 5000 • try to do voluntary work at a local school – ring heads' secretaries direct • see job ads in the *Guardian* on Tuesdays and *The Times Educational Supplement*.

'You've got to be able to be yourself. If you're putting on an act, it won't work. If you've got no personality, then the people in charge of the classroom will be the dominant personalities – and if they're children, then you're in trouble,' says one secondary school teacher.

Whether you're teaching a class of seven-year-olds about magnets, or seventeen-year-olds the principles of a microwave oven, you're helping to shape the nation's most valuable resource: people. Teachers agree there's an enormous 'high' to be got from seeing their pupils achieve something new. But much of the work is a long, hard slog of preparation and marking. Teachers also get a lot of grief from governments who decide to bring in yet another sweeping reform which will mean years of work to implement it properly in the classroom.

You'll do practical teaching experience while you qualify, and then get a job either by word of mouth – a common method – or from job ads in the papers. For many, the first year of teaching is the hardest. Being unused to giving lessons in your subject, you spend long hours preparing material. 'I felt I could have done with more support from my colleagues during that year,' says one English teacher aged twenty-four.

'I think you have to be really committed, know that this is what you want to do,' comments Fionnuala Burke, a twenty-six-year-old history teacher at a school in Stevenage. She adds that it's sensible to build up your own support group of friends and colleagues, for when the going gets tough. And it will! But the subsequent successes of your pupils make the bad times worth while.

VETERINARY NURSE

Working for: veterinary practices in town or country; pharmaceutical companies, research establishments, kennels, zoos.

Salary range: £4,500 to £12,000; maybe more in a pharmaceutical company.

Qualifications: four GCSEs grades A–C or the equivalent, one in English language, one in physical/biological science/maths. Two years of training on the job follow, with exams set by the Royal College of Veterinary Surgeons.

Will suit you if you: are seventeen or over; love animals in a non-sentimental way; are not squeamish; can work with people or alone; are good at handling hairy patients.

Perks: free or subsidised accommodation in some posts.

Pitfalls: dealing with some dangerous animals; you'll never make a million; long, irregular hours including some weekend work.

Future opportunities: become a head nurse, then move on to become an inspector for the RSPCA; join an animal/environment charity, or work with wild animals in a ZOO.

How to get in: • see local vet surgeries for vacancies/voluntary work experience • send a large SAE to the British Veterinary Nursing Association at: BVNA Office, The Seedbed Centre, Coldharbour Road, Harlow, Essex CM19 5AF for info on jobs and where to find them • once you've got a place, contact BVNA again for details of courses/on-the-job training.

'Call, call, call around the surgeries,' says twenty-one-year-old veterinary nurse Emma Bott. Try animal charities too. Voluntary work is the classic route in to this career: you get a few days' work experience, which can turn into odd bits of part-time work at weekends and then, when the next vacancy arises, a job offer.

You have to have a job in order to train as a veterinary nurse. Training lasts a minimum of two years, and consists mostly of learning on the job (it helps enormously to work for a vet, or vets, who actively encourage you in your course) and you'll typically spend half a day each week at a local college. If there is no suitable local college, you're allowed to study at home with extra tuition from the surgery staff. Be persuasive with the staff if necessary: in busy surgeries the junior's training can appear a low priority – but it isn't!

The theory, say veterinary nurses, can seem heavy-going at the time; there's a temptation not to do the homework because the work in the surgery seem so much more real. But the study pays off: you emerge with a grounding of anatomy, biology, the administering of medicines, bandaging, the monitoring of anaesthetics during surgery, and general animal care. Once qualified, your responsibilities extend as far as superficial operations – removing boils and the like, as well as feeding and cleaning out animals on site, and sitting on reception.

VETERINARY SURGEON

Working for: veterinary practices, research establishments, universities, local authorities, zoos, in UK and overseas.

Salary range: £12,500 to £30,000+.

Qualifications: you need 3 or 4 good A Levels in chemistry, physics and biology or similar to get into one of the six British universities (including London, Cambridge, Edinburgh) which each offer places to sixty students per year. It's a five-year course, six in Cambridge. Best to check your A Level choices before you begin them with the veterinary science departments of your preferred universities.

Will suit you if you: are academically able and determined; have a scientific interest in animals, combined with a non-squeamish concern for their welfare; can take hard work; are physically strong.

Perks: once qualified, you'll never be short of a job; prestigious career.

Pitfalls: long, unsocial hours; putting animals down; dangerous beasts!

Future opportunities: excellent. You could be running your own practice by your late twenties, move abroad, or shift sideways with profit into biological or food research. The choice is yours.

How to get in: • for general info and details of the six universities, write to The Royal College of Veterinary Surgeons, 32 Belgrave Square, London SW1X 8QP.

It's 2.30 a.m. and the phone's ringing. A woman on the other end says her cat's been run over . . . can you come and help?

You're used to this. As one of four partners in a town practice, you take it in turns to be on emergency call. 'You do find yourself up during the night, sometimes for things that turn out not to be emergencies at all,' says one vet in her late twenties. 'It's not nine to five, it's a way of life.'

To have reached this stage you will already have cleared two hurdles. First, you will have got one of the heavily coveted 360 places available annually to study in the UK. And, then, you will have completed a gruelling five- or six-year course in which you will have done everything from postmortems (cutting open a dead animal to determine cause of death) and study of anatomy, to work experience in a veterinary practice.

Your first job will probably be in that same or a similar setup – more than half of all vets in the UK work in one of 2,000 practices nationwide. In a town practice, your day's workload will include things like: routine kitten and puppy inoculations; operations on an older pet with suspected cancer; sending blood and urine samples off to a specialist lab for tests; X-raying the leg of a family pony. You might even have to handle the odd exotic pet. In a country practice you'll visit the farms and deal with larger animals on the spot – if you're not fit when you start, you soon will be!

YOGA/MARTIAL ARTS TEACHER

Working for: yourself, doing classes on your own premises or in hired rooms, for local education authority classes, health clubs and farms, hospitals.

Salary range: £3,000 to £20,000 depending on the hours you work.

Qualifications: none required to start with. LEAs and health clubs usually expect you to have a diploma from The British Wheel of Yoga, the biggest UK yoga group – it's a two-year course involving 150 hours of tuition – or a suitable qualification in the martial art of your choice (see addresses below).

Will suit you if you: enjoy the spiritual/physical elements of these Eastern exercises; are a fluent communicator; have a business sense.

Perks: a fit body, fast reflexes, a calm mind and a face free of worry lines!

Pitfalls: not a career for would-be millionaires; you can get rushed off your feet if you say 'yes' to too many classes.

Future opportunities: the interest in yoga, and the more meditative martial arts such as T'ai Chi and Chi Kung, is big in the 1990s, so you should find plenty of clients as you build up your reputation.

How to get in: contact The British Wheel of Yoga, 1 Hamilton Place, Boston Road, Sleaford, Lincs NG34 7ES • information about other Eastern martial arts, from T'ai Chi to Karate, from The Sports Council, 16 Upper Woburn Place, London WC1H 0QP (SAE preferred).

Exercise fads come and go but interest in yoga and martial arts just keeps on growing, according to its teachers throughout Britain. 'With stress levels rising, it's more popular than ever,' reports The British Wheel of Yoga.

Exercising the mind as well as the body makes us happier people. So as a teacher imparting these skills, you'll not only feel the benefits yourself, but will have the satisfaction of seeing visible improvements in the happiness and health levels of your students, who could be private individuals at a lunch or evening class, groups of business people, health farm visitors, hospital patients . . .

As a yoga teacher, you will have undergone a demanding two-year, part-time training under a diploma course tutor in your area. You will have studied the four set course books, which include the *Bhagavad Gita*, and the *Hathayoga Pradipika* (since yoga is a system of physical, mental and spiritual development which originated in India over 3,000 years ago, there's a fair amount of Indian vocabulary still associated with it).

If you're teaching yoga or T'ai Chi (slow, stretching exercises, like ballet in slow motion) you might well divide your day like this: morning classes teaching up to twelve people in a health farm or hospital, lunch class at a local company, evening classes in your own or a hired studio.

It can become a busy and demanding schedule. But as a yoga or martial arts teacher, you should be more able than most to deal with burnout; just meditate your troubles away!

SECTION

TECHNICAL WIZARDRY

From the wheel to the latest computer game, from new food to innovative make-up, everything made by machine was designed by *someone*. Why shouldn't that someone be you?

If you're endlessly curious about how things work; if you enjoy devising solutions to seemingly impossible problems; if you can see how a gadget could be improved, you're a technical wizard in the making.

It's not all pure invention, of course. Technical wizards can also stop planes from crashing into each other, can catch a film director's vision and put it in a can, gather almost limitless information and squeeze it on to a wafer-thin silicon chip.

This area is crying out for new brains. We live in a highly technological age, yet most people find it all a puzzle. So apply some original thinking, and be prepared for the hard slog of research. You never know: you might have the brain-wave of the century!

AIR TRAFFIC CONTROLLER

Working for: Civil Aviation Authority.

Salary: £12,362 to £40,000.

Qualifications: two A Levels and at least five GCSEs grades A–C including English and maths or equivalent, or 'significant aviation experience' and English and maths GCSE. You must: be aged between eighteen and twenty-six; have security clearance before you start work; pass an annual medical, and have reasonable eyesight, coloursight, hearing, and no speech defect.

Will suit you if you: are physically fit, able to work fast, mentally agile, decisive; are good at working both on your own and in a team; are highly safety conscious; can concentrate for long periods; can relate each tiny blip on a screen to hundreds of valuable human lives – without freaking out at the responsibility; can keep a cool head in a crisis.

Perks: the thrill of keeping hundreds of planes up in the air – safely.

Pitfalls: the stress of knowing what a serious mistake could mean.

Future opportunities: you're most likely to be in West Drayton or Prestwick, but you could be posted all over Britain during your career; good potential for promotion.

How to get in: • info from Civil Aviation Authority, CAA House, 45-59 Kingsway, London WC2B 6TE, tel 071-379 7311.

It's been likened to playing 3-D chess, or manipulating a 3-D knitting pattern in the air. Wearing headphones, you sit in a hushed and semi-darkened room, studying radar screens on which a constantly changing pattern of lines and flickering lights must be kept in orderly configurations. Planes are circling in a stack above you, waiting to land, each one 1,000 feet higher than the next. Every plane is represented by a point of light with markings next to it which show its airline code, its altitude (transmitted automatically from the plane) and its destination.

As an approach controller, it's your job to give each flight-deck crew a clear space in which to fly, and to monitor to check that no planes are on a collision course with others taking off and landing. In the Air Traffic Control Centre, a few miles away from the airport, other colleagues monitor aeroplanes flying across England and Wales and the surrounding seas. When a plane leaves your sector, you pass the responsibility on to another controller, in Scotland, Holland, Belgium or France.

When you apply to be an air traffic controller, as long as you satisfy the basic entry requirements, you'll be invited to spend a day taking aptitude tests and seeing what the job entails. People who pass that first stage get an hour-long interview a few weeks later, and the 'We are pleased to tell you . . .' letters go out soon after. You start by learning the theory and practice of air traffic control with the help of simulators, and you'll retrain regularly throughout your career.

CAMERA OPERATOR

Working for: mainly yourself, working to contracts for BBC and ITV companies, satellite and cable, video and film companies.

Salary range: £12,000 to £40,000+; minimum union rate £368.50 per week.

Qualifications: GCSEs in English, maths and physics are useful; you need to show an active interest and technical expertise in film, video or photography, e.g. practical project work at school, or a film/TV/photography course (see FILM EDITOR); good colour vision, hearing and general fitness.

Will suit you if you: have a strong interest in film and photography and an eye for composition; are happy to work anywhere; are a good team member but can also work well alone; are intrepid, go-getting; get on easily with people.

Perks: travel; you're close to the stars.

Pitfalls: being outdoors in all weathers; hard, physical work.

Future opportunities: video production companies and TV are easier to get into than films; once in, if you have the ability and aptitude the work is there: when experienced, you could become a director.

How to get in: • see FILM EDITOR and TV RESEARCHER.

The more obscure the job title, the more junior you are in this industry. The cable basher is responsible literally for dragging heavy camera cables out of the way of studio cameras when they're swinging into a new position. The focus puller adjusts the focus on the camera; the clapper loader claps the slate, loads and unloads the film, keeps a record of all takes.

In practice, they're all camera assistants, and will do one or more of the above jobs depending on the size of the team. The actual tasks vary according to which medium you're in – video or film, you can learn both – and how big the budget is; but broadly, the next stage up is camera operator, where you set up the camera and shoot, choosing your images under the general guidance of the lighting director and the director.

In TV and video companies, the bulk of the work is done by video camera, which requires less crew. Outdoor work often only needs a team of three: one camera, one sound, one presenter; or even two, with sound and camera being operated by the same person. The smaller the crew, the more responsibility you have as a news camera operator, for example, you're as much of a news hound as any journalist: you're adept at tapping into the local grapevine wherever you go, so you hear about the best places to shoot your pictures.

You may like that life so much that you decide to become a stringer (see also FOREIGN CORRESPONDENT), filming news stories from your particular patch abroad, and sending the resulting pictures to TV news agencies and TV stations direct. The best way to discover the direction you want to take is to get work experience in everything you can.

COSMETIC SCIENTIST

Working for: cosmetics companies.

Salary range: £12,000 to £35,000.

Qualifications: a science degree such as chemistry or biochemistry is the route into the interesting research and development positions. Or go into the industry as a technician, with GCSEs in suitable science subjects like chemistry, biology, physics, maths; get a BTEC diploma or study for one year part-time to get the Society of Cosmetic Scientists' Diploma (see below).

Will suit you if you: have a lively and enquiring mind; are creative, analytical; interested in colours and textures; methodical, accurate.

Perks: creating a brand new make-up and seeing it become fashionable; making products that benefit people, like sunscreens.

Pitfalls: if you don't like the idea of testing on animals, you'll need to stay clear of some companies . . . happily, animal-testing is becoming rarer.

Future opportunities: there are many areas in which to specialise, from inventing new products to quality control. Or you could move into management, or marketing . . . or start your own cosmetic company!

How to get in: • shop around for science courses that cover the cosmetics industry • contact firms direct • careers info from The Society of Cosmetic Scientists, Delaport House, 57 Guildford Street, Luton LU1 2NL, tel (0582) 26661 • read *Soap, Perfumery and Cosmetics* for industry info.

'Glug, glug, glug,' goes the thick passionfruit-scented liquid as you mix it in a glass dish. This is one of those careers that little children dream of: it's interesting, it's gloriously messy, and it's wonderfully satisfying when you get it right.

As a cosmetic scientist in research and development, most of your day is spent on the bench, mixing lotions and potions which will eventually be applied to people's faces, bodies, hair or baths. First thing, you have a meeting with your manager, during which you give her an update on work in progress. You then plan out your project with your technicians – they're responsible for ensuring the work area is clear, keeping records and generally helping.

Then the fun begins: mixing fruit, oils and synthetic chemicals into a new product. As a trained chemist or biochemist, you understand how ingredients will react with one another, but it's nevertheless important to test the finished product afterwards; for things like stability, efficacy, safety and so on. This may be done by a colleague.

In Britain we have over 200 cosmetics companies, and we export more cosmetics, toiletries and perfumes than we import, so there are ample opportunities. 'Try to keep the creative side of your personality alive,' advises Jo Warren, who is group scientist for skin care at The Body Shop. 'Scientists can be pushed into routine directions, but it's your career, so go for the type of work *you* want to do.'

ENGINEER

Working for: large and small manufacturing companies in the UK and abroad.

Salary range: start on £10,000 to £18,000, then up to £45,000+.

Qualifications: easiest to get in and on with a degree in engineering for which you usually need A Levels in maths and sciences – two of the many good places are the University of Southampton and Imperial College, London. You can also enter engineering jobs at many different levels without a degree, notably with a BTEC diploma, then train to become a chartered engineer.

Will suit you if you: are curious about how things work and how they could work better; are ingenious, imaginative, problem-solving, patient, enthusiastic, a good communicator, a good team-worker, commercially aware.

Perks: in this job you can look at a plane, a boat, a life-saving piece of medical equipment and think, 'I designed that'; or come up with something really innovative, and get a place in the history books.

Pitfalls: if you make a crucial design mistake, planes may crash, bridges collapse . . . and you'll be responsible.

Future opportunities: no shortage of work – there are currently 2 million engineers employed in Britain, producing 40 per cent of our exports . . . you could become a highly paid manager or engineering consultant.

How to get in: • careers and courses info from The Engineering Training Authority, Engineering Careers Information Service, 41 Clarendon Road, Watford WD1 1HS, freephone 0800 282 167 • see jobs ads in *The Daily Telegraph* and *The Times.*

'The best candidates are the ones who show an active interest in what we do here,' says a senior electronics engineer in aeronautics. 'I like it when interviewees want to be shown around and are curious to see how things work; when they're full of ideas and we find ourselves discussing different ways of tackling a new project.'

Engineering is a blend of creativity and practicality. Virtually everything we use was designed and developed by engineers, and existing technology is being added to at a dizzying speed. In the best companies you'll find a sense of excitement, of doing pioneering work that sometimes seems impossible, until painstaking research mixed with the odd hunch pays off.

Engineering courses last around four years and incorporate practical periods in industry. Individual courses may be general, or may focus on different disciplines such as electronics, mechanical, chemical and civil (building bridges and other structures).

When you're employed you can specialise further: in manufacturing, for example, design engineers turn sketches of cars and chairs into detailed drawings; development engineers produce the first prototypes, and production engineers plan and construct the whole manufacturing process that will enable thousands or millions of identical items to be made.

FOOD TECHNOLOGIST/ SCIENTIST

Working for: food companies, research establishments; environmental pressure groups.

Salary range: £8,000 to £12,000 to start; then up to £40,000.

Qualifications: degree in food technology or related science such as chemistry or microbiology (see below for courses); or degree in science followed by MSc in food; or HND in a science subject. You can sometimes start as an unqualified assistant, and train as you go.

Will suit you if you: have a scientific curiosity in the chemistry of food; are accurate, methodical; can come up with creative ideas; enjoy food!

Perks: free food; you could be the one to develop a cheap new food for famine-struck countries.

Pitfalls: The stress of knowing that if you make a mistake in your calculations, you could cause an outbreak of food poisoning.

Future opportunities: a growth industry – people increasingly want convenience food that's well-made, interesting and safe. There are also jobs in pressure groups, Government bodies, and universities if you tire of the commercial kitchen-laboratory.

How to get in: • careers and courses info from The Institute of Food Science & Technology (UK), 5 Cambridge Court, 210 Shepherd's Bush Road, London W6 7NL, tel 071-603 6316 9.30 a.m.–1 p.m., 2–5 p.m. (A5 SAE preferred).

'Dangerous chemicals found in European wines,' shouts a newspaper headline. Food technologists are the ones who identify something nasty in the bottom of a bottle – and then come up with ways of preventing such contamination in the future.

Food technologists may specialise in food development, or quality control. In the latter, you do systematic chemical trials to measure the quantities of additives and pesticide residues in a food, then come up with schemes to lessen both of these where necessary.

Working for a large supermarket or food manufacturer, you'll be responsible for checking food ranges on a regular basis, monitoring whether there's an unacceptable increase of bacteria or other chemicals. You'll visit your own company's or your suppliers' factories to advise on hygienic practices. And you'll liaise with the packaging departments, to ensure that the food is safely sealed. It's very much science-based, not at all fashion-or 'taste'-led.

Food development is often seen as the more glamorous side of food technology – probably because it's more creative. If you and/or a food buyer has the brilliant idea of putting peanut butter and chocolate spread in the same jar, it's your role to see how the two substances get on in chemical terms, and to suggest improvements to the recipe. Where foods are perishable, you decide how much of which preservative can safely be used. And, of course, you get an invitation to the product launch when your creation is complete!

SOFTWARE ENGINEER/DESIGNER/ PROGRAMMER

Working for: computer manufacturers, software houses, universities, large companies (in-house)

Salary range: £11,000 to £45,000+; some go to £100,000+.

Qualifications: usually, a degree or further degree in mathematics, computing or another numerate subject. Some large companies do recruit non-graduates and train them.

Will suit you if you: have an intellectual interest in dreaming up and developing new computer ideas; have an original mind; are numerate, patient; have high powers of concentration; are happy to work on your own but can also work in a team.

Perks: you could be the designer of the first commercially viable programme that enables personal computers to take dictation . . . or some other marvel.

Pitfalls: in small companies, unscrupulous business partners who stitch you up; in big ones, being just one little cog designing one little part of a gigantic programme . . . with little idea what it's *for*; possibly a risk of Repetitive Strain Injury from continuous tapping at a keyboard.

Future opportunities: limited only by your imagination and skills.

How to get in: • careers info from The British Computer Society, PO Box 1454, Station Road, Swindon, Wilts SN1 1TG, tel (0793) 480269, 9.15 a.m.–5.15 p.m. • study the computing pages of the papers, especially the *Guardian* on Thursdays and *Computing*.

In the enormous and expanding computer industry, this is the starting point that makes everything else possible. As software engineer/designer/programmer (the titles can mean the same or slightly different things according to where you work) you will design the basic languages and programmes which enable ordinary people to use computers as easily as they turn on the television.

You might be developing a fourth generation computer language – something as close to plain, spoken English as is inhumanly possible. Or you might be experimenting with artificial intelligence, teaching a computer first how to learn, and then how to think for itself. Or, you might be designing the actual graphics that the user sees, right down to images of fish or dustbins that fly across some screens while the computer isn't in use.

The irony of being a software engineer is that the first thing you invariably do is turn your computer off. You plan in your head, make sketches on paper. Only when you've thought through the whole concept do you start programming, using an existing language as your base, or writing one from scratch. At its purest, in this job you may never see a non-computer buff. At its most applied, you'll liaise closely with the SYSTEMS ANALYST and redesign programmes to suit a company's very individual requirements.

SYSTEMS ANALYST

Working for: computer consultancies; large companies in-house.

Salary range: £11,000 to £45,000+; some go to £100,000+.

Qualifications: you can go in at any level, but if you have a degree in a numerate subject – computing, maths, business studies, economics – it's a big advantage.

Will suit you if you: are numerate; have an enquiring mind; are practical, a problem-solver; have good people skills; can see the wider picture; are patient but can work to a deadline.

Perks: car and other trimmings that go with consultancy/corporate jobs.

Pitfalls: you'll need diplomacy to deal with people who don't welcome the changes you're bringing to their workplace.

Future opportunities: this field just doesn't stop expanding.

How to get in: • careers info from The British Computer Society, PO Box 1454, Station Road, Swindon, Wilts SN1 1TG, tel (0793) 480269, 9.15 a.m. –5.15 p.m. • study the computing pages of the papers, especially the *Guardian* on Thursday, and *Computing* and *Computer Weekly*.

The systems analyst's job is a bit like painting the Forth Bridge. You go into a company, identify what kind of computer system – the hardware and the software – it needs by talking to the staff and analysing which activities are currently too slow; then you make a report of recommendations, have that report approved by the company's managers, return to your consultancy, source the required hardware, and ask your programmers to develop the necessary software, arrange for the whole thing to be installed, teach the staff how to use it, monitor it . . .

. . . And by the time you've done all that, a new generation of better, faster computers that can do-everything-but-make-the-tea has been invented. Or the company has doubled in size, or its needs have changed. Then, you start again.

Companies all over the UK are still just cottoning on to the use of computers. Others want more sophisticated systems. They will hire your expertise to provide the best, cheapest and most user-friendly machines and programmes.

'When I'm hiring an external consultant, I look for someone who has the skills we're looking for, but also who will get on with my existing team,' says one systems manager in a telecommunications company. And that's the essence of a systems analyst's job: to marry computer technology with people's requirements.

There are plenty of openings in this career, though it may take a few months to get the job you want. Just study the computer pages of the papers and apply to the most active, most happening companies. A common route is to start as a PROGRAMMER, and then progress to analyst. Later, with your combination of people and computer skills, you're in a perfect position for general management – run a large company, or own your own small, swish consultancy.

LETTERS THAT WORK FOR YOU

There are two sorts of letter: the sort that gets its message across to its reader as clearly as a laser beam reaching its target. And the sort that . . . doesn't. The second sort uses five sentences where one will do, hides the priority points among a mass of secondary ones, and says a lot that doesn't need saying.

This chapter gives you the techniques for letters that work – i.e. letters that will help you get the job you want. It covers everything from effective stationery, to how to write clearly and persuasively. And it shows you how to put together the two types of laser beam you'll be sending to employers: letters in response to job ads and on spec letters, where you're simply putting yourself forward as a likely candidate for vacancies that may open up in the next few months. As many companies don't advertise their vacancies, the on spec letter may turn out to be your passport to a brilliant new career.

Although the methods described in this chapter are tried and tested, and will work for you, I don't mean to present them as a rigid formula. There are always other ways of doing things, and it's entirely up to you whether you do what's suggested here, or come up with a method you feel is more suitable for you.

WHAT THE PAPER SAYS

The writing paper you choose sends out its own message to employers. It says a lot about the kind of person you are and it's the first impression they receive.

You want to say you're professional, right for the job, and that you're *you* – not just another hopeful, but an interesting person whose particular qualities will enhance the company in question. This is how you can say it, without even writing a word:

1 Use the kind of writing paper and envelopes that businesses use i.e. A4 white or off-white paper of reasonable quality. 'Conqueror' or 'laid' are suitable for all professions, though some sectors such as architecture use more designerly paper, in which case, you could too, if you wanted to – just ring and ask them to send you some information (invent any excuse) so you can sneakily obtain some samples of their stationery. Use envelopes that match.

2 Just as all business and professional organisations have a letterhead – usually the company's name printed at the top of the sheet, with its address and phone numbers either immediately under the name, or running along the bottom of the page – so can you. It's the clearest way of saying who you are in terms that professional people recognise and respect. And with the abundance of personal computers around today, you may be able to do it for under a fiver, or, certainly, less than £20. Here's how.

If you have access to a computer with different typefaces, such as an Apple Mac – ask around friends and family – you can produce your own artwork for a letterhead. Classic typefaces like Times Roman and Century are good, but play around until you get something that looks professional and you feel is appropriate for you. You might want to use two different typefaces. Look at other business letterheads to give you ideas.

If you don't have access to a computer, just go into any high-street printing shop and explain what you want: artwork for a letterhead which will contain your name and address. Ask them to show you what they can do.

The next stage is to ask a high-street copying shop to produce *photocopies*, not prints (photocopies are cheaper and still look the business) of your letterhead on appropriate blank paper. They'll have a good range of paper from which you can choose, and it only costs a few pence per sheet. Now you have a stack of letter writing paper that will make you feel like a pro before you start.

3 You can type or handwrite your letter – employers say they're happy with either, just as long as it looks neat, doesn't go on for pages and is easy to read. Typed letters look better when the printer ribbon/typewriter ribbon is new or at any rate not wearing out. And write or sign off your letters with a pen that leaves a good impression, such as a fountain pen, or one of the roller-ball letter-writing pens that cost around 90p.

4 Whether you're typing or handwriting your letter, space your words on the page in the same way that professional organisations do. The sample letter at the end of this chapter shows the format. In a nutshell, do it single spaced, with a double space between paragraphs and no indentation of the first line in each paragraph. The name and address of the person you're writing to goes in the top left-hand corner, with the date two spaces below; no punctuation on the address, after the addressee's name at the start of the letter, or after your sign-off at the end.

5 Once you've written your letter and double checked that there are no spelling mistakes (employers hate obvious errors), fold your letter and place it in the envelope like this:

If you've worked in an office, you may think I am stating the obvious, but if you haven't there's no earthly reason why you should know the accepted way of folding letters.

WHAT YOU SAY COUNTS

No one can hand out good letter-writing phrases for every occasion; effective writing simply doesn't work like that. Instead, all you ever have to do is write how you talk, but a little more concisely (making sure your letter and the cv you will enclose with it don't repeat themselves and each other too much). In the process, your own personality will come across. 'Letters that show the applicant's personality always stand out from a dreary pile,' says one publishing director feelingly.

Think about *exactly* what you want to say, and hunt around in your head until you find the right words or images to express it positively. You're not trying to be fancy, just clear. By being clear, you avoid well-worn phrases that turn employers off as they read them.

'One of the things I most hate is reading that someone wants to do this job because they "enjoy dealing with people",' says one personnel manager, whose views were echoed by others I talked to. The plain fact is, every job in the world involves dealing with people to a greater or lesser extent. So by stating a universal truth, you are stating nothing.

RESPONDING TO A JOB AD

An employer has sent a message to you – and perhaps 500 others or more – in the shape of a classified advert in a national or local newspaper, or a trade magazine. Read that ad as carefully as a private detective would, and you can see just how much the company has revealed about itself, and what it expects from its staff. Your challenge is to send back a reply that will reassure the employer that you are the right person for this particular job. It' very easy to do this.

1 Get a clear idea in your own mind of both the nature of the job, and the organisation. Do you want to do this job? The conventional advice today is to apply like crazy for everything you're just about qualified to do. To some extent, there's no harm in practising your application writing skills on a string of poor souls you've got no real intention of joining. But sending applications off willy-nilly is a waste of time and energy. Far better each week to go all out for a handful of jobs you really want to do, than to whack letters off to ten or twenty that you don't have time to think about properly.

If you're unsure what the job entails, you can find out by checking the Top 100 Jobs Directory, by ringing up the personnel department of the company concerned with one or two quick, specific questions, by asking the staff at your reference library (library staff are a wonderful source of free help and information), or by asking at your local careers office. 'I'd like to find out what a behaviourial economist is,' you say, and they'll happily supply you with the basic facts, or the address and phone number of an organisation which knows.

Then make sure you know exactly what the company does. It is clear from the ad? Be devious to get information if you have to. Ring up the personnel department and ask if they have company/careers information they can send you. Book publishers will send out their catalogues, magazine publishers their sales bumph, as long as you sound like you know what you're doing. Regular reading of the business pages of the newspapers and the appropriate trade magazines should give you up-to-date knowledge of your chosen industry.

Of course, you may not want to do *all* this research till you've been called in for an interview, but just enough so you know the bare essentials of what the company does.

2 Next, write down the key words in the ad. It may say, for example, that the company wants someone who is motivated, brimming with ideas, energetic and organised. Make sure these words or artful paraphrases of the same are incorporated in your letter. But keep it simple.

3 Now write your letter in a style that suits you, and suits the type of organisations you're addressing. A bank or building society will expect a more formal approach than a magazine company or a modelling agency. But today clear English is the language favoured by all businesses, and a to-the-point, fresh style works with everyone.

One letter I sent to a woman's magazine, in response to an ad that asked, 'Are you good at x, can you do y and z?', simply began, 'Yes, yes, yes! I can do x and y and I love z.' The reflection of the magazine's own style worked: the editor thought it stood out from the pile and it helped me to get the job.

It can work well if you start as though you're answering a direct question of theirs. Just make sure that in the first or second paragraph you make clear which job you're applying for, and where you saw it advertised. Then back up the rest of your letter with a few salient reasons why you're suitable, and interested, say you're enclosing your cv and look forward to hearing from them. Then sign off.

THE ON SPEC LETTER

You may start off with little idea of the character and style of the organisation in question. Can you find out? Inside knowledge is what you're after. It's not vital; you can write a good letter to anyone right now, but it helps.

So, do you know someone who works there, or in a similar field? Can you ring up the personnel/careers information/marketing department and ask them some quick questions, like what kind of newcomers do they look for, are there any openings now or likely to be in the next few months? You don't even have to say who you are; just say, 'I'm a chartered surveyor (or whatever) and I'm interested in joining a company like yours. Can you tell me . . .?'

At the same time, read the papers and the specialist and trade papers so you know what's going on. Your local library will be able to tell you which trade magazines are published in you chosen area and will stock some of them. Or consult *BRAD*, a publications directory, in the library. Otherwise, buy the relevant magazine from time to time or, as a one-off, ring up the subscriptions department of the publication and ask if you can see a back issue with a view to subscribing. Nice subs departments may send you several.

Your digging around will have given you a general idea of the organisation, and others in its field that you can write to at the same time. It should also, ideally, give you a *handle*, a means of entry.

If a trade magazine or local paper article says Sunset News is setting up a pilot cable television station in your area, say, and you're a recently qualified accountant, a school-leaver interested in accountancy, a would-be electronics engineer, or want to go into personnel or sales (fill in the career of your choice), this is your chance to write to the personnel department at Sunset News head office and say you'd like to be considered for a post in the new branch. Find out the name of the best person to write to by either ringing the switchboard or the personnel department.

This may sound like a lot of hard work, but it really does pay off. You're getting in before the stampede, before others even know there's an opening. Quite simply: you're showing initiative. And there's nothing an employer loves more.

THE APPLICATION FORM

Large organisations often provide an application form for you to fill in – it makes the selection process easier. There's no need to send a letter with it. The only rule is to do exactly what they ask, neatly and clearly. But it still helps enormously to have your cv and perhaps a couple of application letters to hand for your own reference. It means you'll be able to put the salient facts down in a well-ordered fashion, fast.

On page 129 is a sample letter to show the general format. An on spec letter could be pretty similar, but might start: 'I read with interest in this week's *Travel Trade Gazette* that Intrepid Travel is launching a new coach tour service covering Western Europe.' Or, 'I am writing to introduce myself as a candidate for any current vacancies, or any that might develop in the next few months. I graduated . . .'

JOANNE SAUNDERS
3 Maple Road, Bristol, Avon BS6 5NN
Telephone (0272) 03336 (answerphone)

Scarlett O'Hara
Personnel Director
Intrepid Travel plc
43 Waterloo Road
Peterborough PN6 2NQ

23 September 1993

Dear Scarlett O'Hara (*Ms O'Hara if you feel a more formal style is appropriate*)
RE COACH MANAGER, EUROPE (*quick reference so she knows instantly what the letter is about*)
Yes, I have good experience of and qualifications in organising tourist and leisure outings. Yes, I do enjoy a challenge, and I am currently looking for an exciting next step in my career.

I am writing to reply to your advertisement in <u>The Times</u>, 20/9/93, for an area tour manager to take coach tours across Western Europe. I graduated earlier this year with a degree in leisure management at Bristol College. During my training I clocked up a total of four months' experience working as a tour rep for Nordic Coaches in Scandinavia. I have also travelled independently to France, Russia and Spain, and in the process have learned how to deal competently with the unexpected. I also have ample practice at keeping within a travel budget.

I am currently working as a tour guide in Avon, where I take groups on specialist tours for Avon Enterprises plc. I am very keen as the next step in my career to take a post such as coach manager, Europe for Intrepid Travel. I believe your company's international name and wide-ranging itinerary would offer me excellent experience and opportunities to build on my existing leisure management skills.
   The enclosed cv will give you more information on my background. If you would like to know anything else please get in touch. I look forward to hearing from you soon.

With thanks

Yours sincerely

Joanne Saunders

YOUR CV – TICKET TO A NEW CAREER

It's common for high-flyers who've reached the heights of their particular career to keep a one-sheet potted biography to pass on to anyone – headhunters, other companies, journalists – who asks. It's the high-flyers' calling card, and they know that the more places it reaches, the more likely they are to get some attractive new work offer and become even more brilliantly successful.

What works for high-flyers works for us all. Whether you've just left school, college, or are several years into your working career, you can use your curriculum vitae – literally, the story of your life – as an advertisement for yourself. Like any company advertising what it has to offer, you want your cv to reach the largest possible number of suitable people.

It's good sense to keep an up-to-date cv, and make sure you've always got copies to hand. You never know, you might meet someone at a party who is established in the field you want to enter. At the end of the conversation, they ask, or you suggest, that you give them your cv. Pop it in the post the next day with a quick covering note on your headed paper, saying, 'It was nice to meet you at X. Here, as promised, is a copy of my cv for your information. If any suitable positions in your company do become free, I'd love to be considered.'

Since your cv is all about *you*, you're the only one who can decide what to put in it. Employers say it's important that your personality does come through, while keeping it to a clear, professional-looking format.

Here are some basic guidelines to making up an effective cv:

1 *Keep it brief*. 'I have my own cv on one page and I greatly prefer it when prospective employees do too,' states the managing director of an information processing company. 'I don't have time to plough through acres of words. A one-page cv shows that the writer can pare a mass of information down to the essentials – just what I'll want them to do if I take them on and they have to prepare reports,' she adds.

Her view is reflected by other employers. There's no law about this: if you really do feel you have to continue on to a second sheet, that's fine. But with three sheets or more, it becomes less likely that all of it will be read.

2 *Make it noticeable*. Your cv will stand out from the pile if you use your own letterhead (see WHAT THE PAPER SAYS, on page 122) it will look professional, and make you feel the same. If you're a college-leaver competing with thousands of others for a limited number of graduate places, this trick can make the difference between success and failure.

3 *Include all the information employers want*. You'll need: your name, address, telephone number (you don't need to type this again if you're using your own letterhead). You can see what else you'll need on the sample cv on page 133. The 'Interests' heading is optional. If you're at the start of your career, you'll want to put it in; it's an obvious place to indicate your personality. But it becomes less important as your career progresses. Employers yawn if your interests come down to meeting friends, reading, going to the cinema . . . 'Show me someone who doesn't,' they think before tossing your cv on to the rejects pile. They also, however, get worried if your interests are not more or less mainstream: being a member of a fringe political party is all very well, but if you put it in your cv, they may think you'll bring it into the workplace too.

4 *Be positive without lying*. Everyone tells us not to lie on our cvs. I'm bound to say that while researching this book I came across a few free spirits who happily admitted they had lied about salary or experience, and been given very nice jobs as a consequence, thank you very much. Perhaps fittingly, they came from creative areas like music and publishing. On the other hand, one high street bank reports there's been a definite increase in applicants telling untruths – and that they do usually get caught out.

None of us ever *needs* to lie. After eighteen or twenty-five years of living, there's no way that you haven't accrued a string of useful skills. If you're not sure what they are, ask people who know you. So don't be modest, but be honest.

When you write down your history, choose your words carefully, and go for the most favourable impression. If you did voluntary work in a children's camp, can you say you were a group leader, or put it in some other way that conveys a skill or degree of responsibility? Be specific and give examples where you can – it helps the employer to get a more vivid picture of what you've done. For example, if you were a catering assistant in your college holidays or your first permanent job, explain that you cooked, prepared menus, did costings and so on.

5 *Present information clearly*. This means single spacing within sections, dates and qualifications tabulated so they appear as neat, impressive columns, and ample space between the different sections. The simple cv opposite shows one way it could be done so the employer can read it at a glance.

JOANNE SAUNDERS
3 Maple Road, Bristol, Avon BS6 5NN
Telephone (0272) 03336 (answerphone)

CURRICULUM VITAE

PERSONAL DETAILS AND EDUCATION

DATE OF BIRTH: 8.11.70
NATIONALITY: British
MARITAL STATUS: Single

1989-92	Bristol College University of Avon Avon	BSc Hons Leisure management Class: 2:2

My degree in Leisure Management included: environmental studies; social studies; management; accountancy and contemporary business practices. I had work placements in Scandinavia and the Lake District, and wrote a final-year dissertation on ecological influences on the travel industry.

1982-89:	Middleton School Rochdale Lancs	GCE A Levels:	English Geography Economics	A C D
		GCE O Levels:	English Lang Geography English Lit French Maths	A A B B C

WORK

June 92- **Tour guide for Avon Excursions plc**. My work involves taking groups on specialist tours by minibus around Avon: tour subjects include crafts, fine foods and pubs.

June 91-Sept 91: **Tour rep for Nordic Coaches**. Escorting groups of British holiday-makers by coach to the Norwegian Fjords. Assistant to the senior rep, I kept accurate records of all spending, and confirmed bookings.

June 90-Sept 90: I travelled as a **Courier for International Express** to Moscow, then on to St Petersburg. I wrote up an account of my journey, which was published in the *Bristol Evening News*.

OTHER QUALIFICATIONS

Full clean driving licence. Can touch type.

INTERESTS

I have travelled to the USA, France and Spain as well as Russia. In August 91 I went on a sponsored bike ride from St Moritz to Madrid, and raised £800 for medical charities. I also swim, scuba dive and play the guitar.

REFERENCES

On request.

THE PSYCHOLOGY OF SUCCESS

'Of course qualifications matter . . . but if I have to choose between two people – one with the right qualifications and the other with less good ones but the right personality for the job, I'll choose the latter,' was the comment of a personnel officer from a scientific establishment, where you might expect more rigid rules to apply.

I was really surprised at the sheer number of people I spoke to who said, without any prompting, that personality mattered more than qualifications – around 75 per cent altogether. They weren't saying they never look for qualifications, just that the combination of the right personality with acceptable certificates is better than being a boffin.

Even a barrister echoed this view: 'I'd say to get a tenancy in chambers today, you do pretty well have to have a first or a 2:1, but you also need to be generally clued up about the world . . . to be able to communicate. A candidate with a brilliant degree who can't interact with people will be rejected in favour of the second-class degree-holder who can.'

The truth is, even when the glossy company recruitment brochures state a candidate must have 'Two good A Levels' or 'a good degree', they don't necessary mean what they say. They're always willing to be charmed by a sparky candidate: 'We'd probably accept someone with a third-class degree if personality-wise they seemed right for us,' confessed a personnel manager at a large clearing bank.

Happily, it takes far less time to acquire the knack of projecting your personality than it does to study for a degree. So here are some strategies to give you the psychological edge to get the job you want. They'll all contribute to making you look and sound natural, interested, informed, with a real sense of being yourself, while being able to fit into a team – which is what employers really want. Being yourself does not, thank heavens, mean putting in a flawless performance. If you make mistakes, don't worry about them, learn by them, and move on. And think of a fluffed interview as good practice for the next one where you'll now stand a better chance of scooping the job.

TURN YOUR JOB HUNT INTO A PROJECT IN ITS OWN RIGHT

If you're currently not working, make your search for a career into a full-time job. If you are working, allocate set times each day or each week to your search. Give yourself a list each day or week of things to do – and then do them. Organise the paperwork – an expanding file, made of cream card (about £7 from W H Smith) is a good investment. Make sure you have the stationery you need for the right professional image (see WHAT THE PAPER SAYS, Pp. 122–3).

And then generate as much activity as you can comfortably deal with. The more activity you generate, the more comes back to you. This does not mean sending off an avalanche of letters, though you will be a prolific letter writer. It means targeting your applications strategically.

MAKE USE OF CONTACTS

Mention what you're doing to friends, family, older family friends and other people you meet, to see if they have any contacts in the industry you're targeting. It is amazing how many contacts each of us has, if we only start telling other people (current bosses usually excluded) what we're up to. Ask if you can be introduced to any industry contacts that come up through friends etc. and whether you can talk to them, on the phone, in their office, over a drink.

One person who recently did this was Diane, a chartered surveyor of twenty-five. 'I had drawn up a short-list of companies I would have liked to move to. I met up with a fairly senior surveyor I knew through friends. He gave me the low-down on each company I had listed, and in each case suggested a particular person for me to write to. I did so, mentioning my contact's name. All 12 wrote back to me within a month. Four offered me interviews, and I've now accepted a job offer from one of them.'

Making use of contacts gives you an advantage over others – but it's not an unfair one. Look upon it as another form of research; because if you want up-to-date knowledge of the career you're going for, there's nothing better than getting it from someone who's already there.

DON'T LET THE REJECTIONS GET YOU DOWN

Self-employed author Sarah Litvinoff says every author she knows has had many more rejections than acceptances for their book proposals. 'It goes with the job.' And the same is true whichever field you're hoping to enter.

The trick is not to take it personally. *Everyone* gets rejection letters (even though some like to pretend they don't). For example, those I spoke to about television jobs agreed that no one ever gets into the BBC on their first interview. 'You have to show you're keen, by applying again and again,' said one TV researcher who now works in BBC news.

All those 'We are sorry to tell you' letters are best considered as useful, free market research. Read them objectively for feedback that can be used to improve future applications. A succession of standard rejections means that you need to reconsider your strategy: perhaps your cv needs pepping up, so that it emphasises more clearly the experiences and achievements that are relevant to the industry in question.

Perhaps you could try sending out more letters on spec, or making a few phone calls to personnel departments. By experimenting with different methods, you'll find that some produce better results than others. Some rejection letters, on the other hand, give encouragement: relish them.

The best cure for the rejection blues is a steady roll of activity. If you've always got at least one application out, there's something hopeful happening all the time.

STAY POSITIVE

Three years ago Sarah, then twenty-three, was fired from a new job. Not surprisingly, she was shattered. But she picked herself up and started job-hunting. She showed me her first letters. As an outsider, I could spot the minor key that ran through them – they sent out the signal: 'I have been occupationally mugged. I'm a victim . . . and now I'm applying to you for a job.'

The brutal fact is that negative letters produce a negative response. Positive letters are much more likely to produce a positive one. The idea is to come across as someone who is not desperate, who is busy and successful (you can always seem to be doing *something*: voluntary work, a bar job in a themed restaurant . . .) and is simply looking for the next step in their career, whether it's immediate or perhaps in a year's time.

Sarah switched the tone in her letters to a major key. She presented herself as a positive, motivated, enthusiastic and able worker, too busy progressing to look back in anger. By doing so, she immediately started feeling that she *was* all those things. Within four weeks she had an excellent new job, and she's still flourishing in the same company today.

• It's extremely useful to recharge your positive batteries by collecting inspiring role models, strong quotes and lyrics, with the aim of reminding yourself that if others can do it, so can you. When, about a third of the way through writing this book, I began to feel seriously fazed by the sheer enormity of the task, I received some careers information from the British Wheel of Yoga which instead of itemising a list of the academic qualifications they required, contained this statement: 'Set your heart in one place and nothing is impossible for you.' It had a beneficial effect: I used it as a switch to turn a negative attitude into an 'I can do it', positive one. When we start looking, we find the world is full of encouraging people and inspiring words to help us turn our dreams into reality.

CONFIDENCE TRICKS

• If, when talking to a prospective employer on the phone or in an interview, your voice goes squeaky or wobbly with nerves, adopt this simple technique:

'Give yourself the note to breathe,' advises Patsy Rodenburg, author of *The Right To Speak*, and Royal National Theatre voice coach who is renowned for empowering people through body language exercises. She adds that slow, deep, regular breathing helps the voice to come out in an uncluttered column of air, which is what makes the difference between a squeak and a calm, naturally carrying voice. To maintain that uncluttered column of air, bend down and touch your toes before standing up and making a difficult phone call; talk standing up or, at any rate, not hunched over your stomach. And remember to breathe deeply and evenly during conversations. Ragged breath produces a ragged voice.

• Use this meditational technique in the morning before an interview:

Sit quietly and comfortably, breathing evenly. Close yo⌐ eyes. Imagine the air you breathe in is bringing positive, recharg ing energy, and good thoughts about yourself and how well you're going to do. As the air goes out, imagine it sweeps away all negative and defeatist thoughts. Spend a few minutes doing this, and you should feel calm, strong, peaceful and ready.

THE BEST INTERVIEW EVER

Seven strategies to lead to a superb interview – and a tempting job offer:

1 Go into it prepared. You will have run through a range of likely questions beforehand, including some stinkers, and you'll have answers ready. You will have researched the company, and perhaps know a few topical things you can artfully bring into the interview to show you're clued up.

You will already have given them your cv, but psychologically it can be very effective to turn up at the interview with something else for them: perhaps a proposal for a particular project, typed on one or two sheets of paper. This gives the subliminal message that you are someone who produces the goods – that in future meetings as an employee of the company you will turn up with reports completed on time, well-presented and well-done.

2 Wear something that is comfortable, professional, appropriate for the job you're going for – a suit that is great for a bank might put off a music company, unless, perhaps, it was imaginatively jazzed up – and reflects *you*. Borrow the model's trick mentioned in the Top 100 Jobs Directory: tell yourself that the outfit looks stunning and your body language will change as a result. If you act as though you look good and feel confident, people respond to those signals.

3 Shake hands on introducing yourself. That physical contact makes the interviewer register you more fully – but it's only effective if it's firm and decisive without going over the top. Floppy paws suggest a passive employee; people in the City shake hands more vigorously. If you're facing a panel, forget about shaking all those hands: just smile, look at them, say hello and introduce yourself. And make a stab at remembering every-one's name by repeating each one when you hear it.

4 Establish good eye contact. Look directly at interviewers, with-out glaring fixedly, or feeling uncomfortable about it. You'll give the impression that you're interested in them, interested in the job, and that you're on the level. You only have to think how difficult it is to look someone in the eye when you don't like them, to see how expressive eye contact – or lack of it – can be.

5 Body language gives away our true feelings – and it's amazing how quickly it changes when we're feeling nervous. *Think* your-self into enjoying the situation: you're rising to a pleasurable challenge and feeling pretty relaxed about it, though alert; and your body movements will tend to reflect those feelings and reinforce them. Sit straight and openly, not hunched up, not masking bits of your face or body with your hands.

6 When questions get seriously tough, and you get heated, step outside yourself and observe the whole interview as though you were a sociologist studying the behaviour of a group of apes (as long as this doesn't make you laugh!). That's what much of human behaviour comes down to anyway. You'll be able to see, then, that the interviewer is deliberately trying to wind you up/intimidate you. As long as your feelings aren't engaged, you can choose how to respond. If the question is overly personal, you can gracefully decline to answer, give them a question back, or talk about the personal subject in general terms. Don't act fazed; tell yourself you're not.

7 Salary talk shouldn't start too early, but if things have gone well, you can bring it up in a pleasant, open, non-aggressive way. Be prepared to negotiate: in the world of work, nothing is fixed despite what they try to tell you. So if you're offered £11,500, ask if it can be raised to £12,000, or say you were think-ing of £14,000 and negotiate down if that seems more appropriate. But keep it pleasant; you're on the same team – or you will be shortly.

You don't have to come up with an instant reason why you think the job you'd do is worth the extra sum (though you should have a reason handy if they look unconvinced). It's surprising how often people will budge from their original offer. And they will respect you afterwards as someone with a good negotiating head on her shoulders – a useful asset to their company.

SHAPE YOUR OWN CAREER

There is a regular battery of advice directed at all of us – by teachers, parents, friends, colleagues, careers advisers, bosses – 'If I were you I'd do this . . .'; 'you'll never get a job as that . . .'.

Much of the advice is useful, and a lot of it is garbage. It's up to you to decide what you're going to do, up to you to shape your career as *you* want. Every single successful person was told somewhere along the line that she didn't have what it takes to achieve her dreams. When you're given useless advice like that, forget it. Move on – keep positive.

Watch out, too, for the bullshit factor. This is how to spot it: while listening to advice, step into the adviser's shoes, and ask yourself clear-headedly, what's in it for them? You do, sadly, get colleagues and bosses who advise against a promising career because the idea of change unsettles them: if you go shooting off and having fun in a stimulating new career, they may feel like nowhere people in comparison.

At the same time, people higher up the career ladder can be very helpful – if you ask them specific questions. Most careers officers will do their best to give you further information, though their effectiveness can vary (most of us have received pieces of official careers advice that seem to belong to a parallel dimension, not applying to the real world of work). So you have to be a dogged researcher, asking and asking different people until you find out what you need to know.

Because, in the end, it's up to you. You can have the career you want, if you go for it. The only certain thing is that if you don't try for something, you definitely won't attain it. So get informed, get active, apply all your wide-ranging powers to the challenge. And you'll step into the job for you.

INDEX

ACKNOWLEDGEMENTS

A total of over 500 people told me about their careers for this book, often squeezing time from busy schedules to do so. There are far too many to mention here, but a heartfelt thanks to each of them for offering up valuable information on what it's really like to get in and on in each job, and for showing how enjoyable the right career can be.

Warm thanks also to Mandi Norwood and Tara Barker at *Company Magazine* for coming up with the idea, to Denise Bates and Joanna Sheehan at Ebury for turning it into a reality, and to my agent Elizabeth Roy for her timely encouragement. And a very special thanks to my partner Steven Day, for all his brilliant support.

Quote by Edward de Bono reproduced with permission from Penguin Books Ltd; taken from his book, *Handbook for the Positive Revolution*, Viking, 1991.